THE GREAT SALSA BOOK

THE GREAT SALSA BOOK

MARK MILLER

with
Mark Kiffin
and
John Harrisson

Photography by
Valerie Santagto

Ten Speed Press
Berkeley

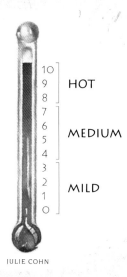

10
9
8 — HOT
7
6
5 — MEDIUM
4
3
2
1 — MILD
0

JULIE COHN

TEMPERATURE SCALE: All salsas are numbered according to this subjective heat reference, 10 being the hottest and 0 being the mildest.

To Lucy, the spice of my life

Cover and book design by Fifth Street Design, Berkeley, California.

Photo styling by Fifth Street Design.

Chile photos on cover by Lois Ellen Frank.

Our thanks to John Trejo, Miles James, Shale Wills, and Ken Rissolo for their invaluable assistance with recipe testing. We are grateful also to Cindy Trejo for her logistical help and for all the errands we asked her to run.

Props provided for photographic sets by Paulette Tavormina.
Additional props, Valerie Levine

We would like to thank the following businesses and individuals for allowing us to use their artifacts, ceramics, dinnerware, textiles and decorations in our photos: Mexican artifacts, courtesy of Barbara and Robin Cleaver; Mexican decorations courtesy of Adevina Coffee Cantina, Santa Fe; dinnerware courtesy of Cookworks, Santa Fe; dinnerware and pottery courtesy of Santa Fe Pottery; artifacts courtesy of Johnson and Benkert Gifts and Antiques; Mexican folk art courtesy of Jackalope; porcelain bowls by Heidi Loewen.

Also thanks to Brenton Beck, Valerie Santagto, Paulette Tavormina, and, of course, Mark Miller for allowing us to use their treasures in this project.

TEN SPEED PRESS
Post Office Box 7123
Berkeley, California 94707
www.tenspeed.com

Library of Congress Cataloging-in-Publication Data

Miller, Mark Charles, 1949—
    The great salsa book / Mark Miller, with Mark Kiffin and John Harrison : photography by Valerie Santagto.
        p.   cm.
    ISBN-13: 978-0-89815-517-4
    ISBN-10: 0-89815-517-7
    1. Salsas (Cookery)   I. Kiffin, Mark. II. Title.
    TX819.S29M54   1994
    641.8 114 dc20   94-1839
                            CIP

Manufactured in China

19 20   10 09 08

≈ CONTENTS ≈

≈ **INTRODUCTION** ≈
~~~~~~~~~~

Salsa. *1.* a spicy sauce of tomatoes, onions, and hot peppers. *2.* popular music of Latin American origin that has absorbed characteristics of rhythm and blues, jazz, and rock.— ***Merriam-Webster's Collegiate Dictionary***

Whether you're referring to the music or the food, say "salsa," and you immediately convey a sense of revelry, happy times, and fun. It is probably no coincidence that the word stands for both the rhythmic, brassy music and for the colorful, *picante* South-of-the-Border condiment, as they share the same festive spirit. In musical terms, salsas can raise the tempo of any food, speed up its flavors and beat, and give it soul. In culinary terms, the music is tantalizing and spicy.

Of course in this book, I'm speaking of salsa as condiment, and a very popular condiment it has become over the last few years. In fact, sales have boomed so much that salsa has pushed King Ketchup out of the top-selling spotlight in the North American condiment market. This trend reflects the culinary acculturation of the American people, and the efforts of food professionals to satisfy the demand for new taste experiences. Larger numbers of people than ever before are growing up with multi-ethnic foods in the kitchen, a pattern reflected in a new "national table." Ethnic foods of all kinds have become immensely popular, and in any large cosmopolitan city one can find a dazzling variety of ethnic cuisines. And now the non-European cultures have become a major influence on the way we eat and the foods available in stores and restaurants.

Thanks to the popularity of the Southwestern, Tex-Mex, and Mexican cuisines all across the United States, almost everyone is familiar with the typical tomato-onion-chile salsa — the kind that is served as an accompaniment to chips or as a garnish. But as people become more familiar with other ethnic foods, they discover that salsas are a major feature on the culinary landscape all over the world, that it doesn't begin and end with *salsa fresca*. There are sambals from Southeast Asia, kim chee from Korea, tsukemono from Japan, raitas and chutneys from India, tabbouleh from the Middle East, pesto and tapenade from the Mediterranean, and harissa and other spice and groundnut mixtures in parts of Africa. They may assume different forms, and be made from different ingredients, but the concept is the same.

In recent years, we have seen a blossoming of the number of "fusion" restaurants that combine different cuisines, using techniques and ingredients that cut across cultures. Salsas have become an important part in these settings, and out of this has come new culinary ideas and new taste experiences that take us beyond strictly ethnic boundaries.

The growing popularity of salsas is also due to an increasing awareness of nutritional issues. We are returning to a healthier way of eating: Grains, fruits, legumes, vegetables, and organic produce of all kinds now play a larger part in our diets. Recent dietary recommendations and advocacy of the new Food Pyramid have spurred on the demand for foods with less fat and animal protein. Consumers are learning that there really is no need for creamy sauces with excessive amounts of sugar, stabilizers, and additives for food to be appealing. This is where salsas can shine, as they can provide excitement and flavor in a healthful and natural form; they can make a prudent diet fun and tasty.

Another major factor behind the appeal of salsas is their freshness, a culinary catchword for the '90s. The simplicity and ease with which they can be made at home and in restaurants alike ensures their freshness and integrity. They also allow you more control over your culinary destiny as you can season your food to your own taste. With salsas, you can make the dish dance a little faster — or a little slower — as you wish. By varying the amount of chiles and other spices and the overall balance of ingredients, you can create sedate salsas that are like waltzes, and others that are more like flamencos. Salsas can perk up conversations as well. Try serving a very *picante* salsa cold, or a salsa with unexpectedly juxtaposed ingredients — it'll get people talking!

Composing A Salsa

The principal notes that make up a salsa "composition" and give it definition and interest are the flavor and texture of the basic ingredients, and their color, sweetness, acidity, and heat. And then there are the aromatic herbs and spices you use to complete the salsa. The creativity in composing salsas stems from playing on the counterpoints of these various notes. For example, combining strong flavors (such as anchovy and rosemary), or contrasting pungent and subtle tones (cumin and wild mushrooms); trading off sweetness and heat (ripe mango and serrano chile), sweet and sour tastes (strawberries and balsamic vinegar), or plain and fancy ingredients (potatoes and caviar).

In creating a new salsa, I find it helps to think about ingredients having different pitches, speeds, and intensities. For example, adding acidic fruit juices or vinegar speeds up the beat of a salsa and quickens flavor perception. It helps a salsa balance heavier, slower foods, such as dark meat, grains, or other proteins. Chiles and aromatic herbs such as cilantro or lemon grass can provide the high notes. Examples of foods that contribute the low bass notes include tomato paste, cooked beans, apples, or potatoes; any of these will slow down the rhythm of a salsa.

I am often asked about the difference between salsas and sauces. While there are no absolutes, I like to characterize salsas as a combination of raw, cooked, or partially cooked ingredients that are put together to form a harmonious chord. In a good salsa, each component retains its own taste, texture, and personality so that each bite will contain a myriad of flavors and a kaleidoscope of textures. In a sauce, on the other hand, all the ingredients are usually cooked together to create a single texture and a more homogeneous taste.

My Love Affair with Salsas: A Brief History

I've often thought about how my passion for salsas was aroused. I think it all started innocently enough, with mustard, onions and relish on hot dogs; molasses on beans; honey on bread; lettuce, tomato and ketchup on burgers; and chocolate syrup on ice-cream. But I do recall that, as a young child, instead of putting a polite spoonful of my grandmother's piccalilli on a cracker, I'd take the spoon to the jar and eat it straight, never mind the crackers! I got through a lot of jars of piccalilli that way.

As I grew older, I couldn't get enough flavor in my food, and the more intense the tastes, the better. I didn't care for "traditional" food presentations favored by the grown-ups around me: I was a "taste rebel," and I just wanted to do my own thing. With apologies to the voyagers in the Starship Enterprise, you might say I was on a "taste trek;" my mission was to seek out new taste sensations and to boldly go where no palate had gone before!

I was still too young to know or care whether my preferences were nutritionally correct (mostly, they weren't). I simply jumped in with my mouth open, pushing new taste barriers, just as other people consume salsas, so they tell me, to "push the envelope" of their own taste experiences. You might say (pun intended), that I did so with relish.

Later on, when I started cooking for myself, I realized I could create my own flavor combinations and control the ingredients to achieve the results I wanted. Soon after that I began my personal campaign against dull, boring food, a campaign that I wage to this day! All too often, people have low expectations of food and don't think about the flavor or content of what they're eating. Many rely on familiar "comfort foods" that are overly processed and contain too much fat, salt, or sugar. Sometimes the most exciting thing about the food they eat is the packaging, which is a sad thought.

The progression I made on my culinary voyage was not unique, at least in its early stages. I began by learning about the food of New England, where I grew up, and then I explored other American regional fare, through travel. As an impressionable teenager, I avidly watched Julia Child's TV programs and read food magazines. Then I traveled abroad, at first to France and Italy, later on to North Africa, Central and South America, and Asia, which reinforced my interest in foods with strong flavor and character. I vividly recall my forays into the local markets and native restaurants and cafes. Whether they were Moroccan, Indian, Asian, or South American, the foods I sampled all seemed to include some form of spicy condiment similar to salsa. They influenced my culinary education and I was to draw inspiration from them in later years as a food professional.

It also helped that I went to college in Berkeley — a hotbed of revolution, both political and culinary — and lived in the Bay Area for many years. San Francisco is a city composed of a number of ethnic neighborhoods with excellent food markets, and I haunted them all. It was in the Bay Area that I began my professional career as a chef. I began at Chez Panisse and then opened the Fourth Street Grill, my first restaurant in Berkeley. I started experimenting with salsas as an alternative to the traditional beurre blanc or heavier cream sauces. In the beginning, I borrowed mostly from the Latin and Mediterranean cuisines: pineapple salsa served with grilled swordfish; black bean-orange salsa with tuna; grilled chicken with gremolata, an Italian salsa made with fresh parsley, marjoram and basil, garlic, lemon zest, olive oil and capers; *salsa fresca* served with grilled steaks; all became signature dishes at the restaurant. People loved them, and enjoyed participating in my taste experiments.

In 1980, when I opened my next Berkeley restaurant, the Santa Fe Bar and Grill, I extended this repertoire to feature a wide range of Southwestern and Caribbean salsas, and began experimenting with smoked chiles, too. These new salsas were also received with overwhelming enthusiasm. Then, when I moved to Santa Fe and opened Coyote Cafe in 1987, the role of salsas in my modern Southwestern cuisine took much more of a center stage, as it does to this day.

The recipes that follow are a compendium representing almost 20 years of work with the concept of salsas. You'll find some old familiar favorites, and some brand new creations, salsas that are relatively tame, and others that walk on the wild side. Some are sweet, most are somewhat *picante*, and all are full of personality. Whatever your mood, whatever you're cooking, whatever you have on hand, you'll find a salsa recipe in this book to match. So make every day a salsa day — and down with dull, boring food!

Some Tips on Creating Your Own Salsas

❖ In general, the only equipment you'll need will be a sharp knife, a cutting board, a blender, a food processor, and grater. If possible, invest in a Japanese grater or a mandolin. Either would be an invaluable tool for preparing salsas.

❖ Always choose the freshest and ripest of ingredients. They may cost more, but they'll have the truest flavors. Buy fruit and vegetables that are heavy for their size and that look good (if it looks or feels crisp and crunchy, it probably will be), then use them as soon as possible. Never use limp ingredients.

❖ If you're not familiar with any of the techniques or ingredients called for, consult the Cooking Techniques section and Glossary at the back of the book. The Sources list provides mailorder suppliers for ingredients you might not be able to find locally.

❖ Avoid dusty or faded spices. Use fresh herbs; preferably, grow them yourself, in a window box if need be. You can grow a variety of chiles at home in pots and they make very attractive ornamental plants. (By the way, consult my *Great Chile Book* if you don't recognize some of the chiles called for — it shows you what they look like and describes their characteristics.)

❖ Use good-quality oils and vinegars and use up oils within a few months as they will deteriorate with age.

❖ Using vinegars or the natural acids in citrus fruit juices for flavor enhancement reduces the amount of salt and sugar you'll need, which is healthier for you.

❖ Use raw, unrefined sugar instead of granulated sugar when possible.

❖ Ingredients in salsas should retain their own character.

❖ Whenever appropriate, cut the different ingredients in a salsa to the same size. Usually, the smaller they're cut, the more interesting the salsa will be. Each spoonful should contain a little of all the ingredients.

❖ Where possible, include ingredients with a variety of colors.

❖ Fresh fruit salsas tend to be the most fragile and should be used as quickly as possible. Allow all other salsas to sit for 30 minutes or longer before use so the flavors marry and any "sharp corners" get rounded out.

✤ If you need to make a salsa ahead of time, choose one that has precooked or partially cooked ingredients — it'll hold up better.

✤ Be flexible. Go to the store with a back-up recipe in case the ingredients for your first-choice salsa are unavailable or don't look fresh.

✤ Hold a salsa party. Grill some chicken or fish and ask each of your guests to bring a different salsa. You can even suggest one of the recipes from this book! Or, if you're feeling energetic, make five to ten different kinds of salsa and try them out on your friends. Prepare some different tidbits, such as chips, tacos, or salads, or grilled foods. Your friends will love you for it!

≈

When people think "salsa," they usually think first of the familiar tomato and its green counterpart, the tomatillo. There's something about red, ripe, juicy tomatoes and green, tart tomatillos that makes them a great starting point for any number of appealing salsa recipes. Fortunately for dedicated salsa-makers, these two ingredients are readily available year-round in most parts of the country.

≈

TOMATO
AND
TOMATILLO
S A L S A S

≈TOMATILLO SALSA VERDE≈

1 pound tomatillos (about 15), husked, rinsed, and roughly chopped
3 serrano chiles, with seeds
¾ cup fresh cilantro leaves (1 bunch)
2 tablespoons fresh lime juice
1 teaspoon sugar
1 teaspoon salt

Place all the ingredients in a food processor or blender, and purée.

Serving suggestions: An all-purpose salsa verde; especially good with tortilla chips, most seafood, and eggs.

Yield: About 2 cups   **Heat:** 5

≈SALSA ROMANA≈

8 Roma tomatoes (about 1 pound), diced
3 tablespoons finely diced red onion
¾ cup loosely packed julienned basil leaves
1 teaspoon finely minced garlic
3 tablespoons extra-virgin olive oil
1 teaspoon salt

Thoroughly combine all the ingredients together in a mixing bowl. Allow to sit at room temperature for 1 hour before serving.

Variation: Add 1 tablespoon balsamic vinegar for a tarter flavor. True Italians would double the salt.

Serving suggestions: With pasta, fish, or on grilled bruschetta or pizza.

Yield: About 3 cups   **Heat:** 0

〰〰〰〰〰

≈SUN-DRIED TOMATO SALSA≈

¾ cup sun-dried tomatoes (in oil), drained, and finely minced
2 anchovy fillets (in olive oil), drained and finely minced
½ cup extra-virgin olive oil
1 teaspoon finely minced garlic
2 tablespoons finely minced roasted shallot
2½ teaspoons finely minced fresh thyme leaves
4 teaspoons finely minced fresh basil leaves
1 tablespoon finely minced fresh Italian parsley
Large pinch of cayenne powder
2 teaspoons freshly ground black pepper
1 teaspoon sherry vinegar

Thoroughly combine all the ingredients together in a mixing bowl.

Serving suggestions: With grilled lamb, pasta, or as a sandwich spread.

Yield: About 1 cup   **Heat:** 1

〰〰〰〰〰

GOLDEN TOMATO, GINGER, AND CHIPOTLE SALSA

3 yellow tomatoes (about 1 pound), roughly chopped
1 chipotle chile en adobo
1 tablespoon chopped fresh ginger
1 teaspoon roasted garlic
1 tablespoon Coyote Cocina Howlin' Hot Sauce
or other Scotch bonnet chile sauce
1 tablespoon fresh lime juice
½ teaspoon sugar
½ teaspoon salt

In a food processor or blender, purée 2 of the tomatoes, the chipotle chile, and ginger. Add the remaining tomato and all of the other ingredients and pulse just enough to create a roughly blended mixture. Be sure to leave the salsa somewhat chunky.

Variation: Substitute 1 additional teaspoon Howlin' Hot Sauce or other yellow Scotch bonnet sauce or 1 teaspoon habanero chile sauce for the chipotle chile.

Serving suggestions: With grilled tuna, swordfish, pork, or duck.

Yield: About 2 cups   **Heat:** 7

≈ SALSA MEXICANA ≈

2 tablespoons finely diced white onion
8 Roma tomatoes (about 1 pound), diced
2 serrano chiles, finely diced, with seeds
2 tablespoons finely chopped fresh cilantro leaves
1 teaspoon sugar
1 teaspoon salt
1 tablespoon fresh lime juice

Place the onion in a strainer, rinse with hot water, and drain. Thoroughly combine all the ingredients in a mixing bowl. Add a little more sugar if the tomatoes are acidic, but make sure the salsa does not taste of sugar. Chill in the refrigerator for at least 30 minutes before serving to allow the flavors to combine.

Serving suggestions: An all-purpose salsa; especially good with tortilla chips or grilled meats.

Yield: About 2 cups   **Heat:** 4

≈ TOMATILLO-AVOCADO SALSA ≈

1 pound tomatillos (about 15), husked, rinsed, and roughly chopped
1 avocado, peeled, pitted, and roughly chopped
1 serrano chile, with seeds
¾ cup fresh cilantro leaves (1 bunch)
2 tablespoons fresh lime juice
1 teaspoon salt

Place all the ingredients in a food processor or blender, and purée.

Serving suggestions: With tortilla chips, or with chicken.

Yield: About 2¼ cups   **Heat:** 2

FIRE-ROASTED TOMATO CHIPOTLE SALSA

1/4 cup plus 1 tablespoon virgin olive oil
1/2 onion, peeled and chopped
2 pounds Roma tomatoes, blackened
4 teaspoons finely minced roasted garlic
1/2 cup minced fresh cilantro leaves
4 chipotle chiles en adobo, chopped
1/4 cup red wine vinegar
1 tablespoon salt
1 teaspoon sugar

Heat a tablespoon of olive oil in a sauté pan over medium heat until lightly smoking, add the onion, and sauté until caramelized, about 10 minutes. Transfer the onion, half the blackened tomatoes, and garlic to a food processor or blender, and pulse until finely chopped but not puréed. Add the cilantro and chipotle chiles, and pulse again to mix.

Peel, seed, and chop the remaining pound of tomatoes, and fold in together with the remaining 1/4 cup olive oil, vinegar, salt, and sugar.

Variation: Substitute 2 pounds of tomatillos for the tomatoes. Husk and rinse the tomatillos, and blacken them before using.

Serving suggestions: An all-purpose salsa; especially good with tortilla chips or red meats.

Yield: About 4 cups   **Heat:** 5

WILD MUSHROOM AND
SUN-DRIED TOMATO SALSA

4 ounces morel and/or chanterelle mushrooms, or 1 portobello mushroom
3 tablespoons extra-virgin olive oil
½ cup onion, diced
3 Roma tomatoes, blackened
1 cup sun-dried tomatoes (in oil), diced
3 tablespoons roasted red bell pepper, peeled, seeded, and diced
2 teaspoons minced roasted garlic
1½ tablespoons minced fresh Italian parsley
2 teaspoons balsamic vinegar
2 tablespoons fresh lemon juice
1 teaspoon salt
1 teaspoon freshly ground black pepper

Brush the mushrooms with 1 tablespoon of the oil and grill until tender. Cut into ¼-inch dice and transfer to a mixing bowl. Heat another tablespoon of oil in a skillet and sauté the onion for 5 minutes over medium heat. Add to the mixing bowl. Cut the blackened tomatoes in half and squeeze out and discard the seeds and juice. Chop and add to the mixing bowl. Add the remaining tablespoon of olive oil and the remaining ingredients and combine thoroughly.

Serving suggestions: With pasta or as a pizza topping.

Yield: About 2 cups   **Heat:** 0

ROASTED TOMATO
AND MINT SALSA

8 Roma tomatoes (about 1 pound), blackened
1 small serrano chile, blackened, finely minced, with seeds
1 orange, peeled, seeded, and cut into sections
3 tablespoons loosely packed chopped mint leaves
1 tablespoon extra-virgin olive oil
2 tablespoons fresh orange juice
1 heaping tablespoon minced orange zest
1 teaspoon sugar
½ teaspoon salt

Cut the tomatoes in half and squeeze out and discard the seeds and juice. Chop the pulp and thoroughly combine with the remaining ingredients in a mixing bowl.

Variation: For a hotter salsa, add 1 minced chipotle chile en adobo.

Serving suggestions: With lamb or halibut.

Yield: About 2 cups   **Heat:** 1-2

≈ OVEN-ROASTED TOMATO ≈
SALSA

8 Roma tomatoes (about 1 pound), oven-roasted and diced
1 tablespoon minced roasted shallots
$\frac{1}{2}$ teaspoon minced roasted garlic
3 tablespoons minced pitted Niçoise or Kalamata olives
4 teaspoons minced capers
$\frac{1}{2}$ teaspoon minced fresh rosemary
$\frac{1}{2}$ teaspoon salt
Pinch of cayenne powder
Zest of 1 lemon, finely minced
1 tablespoon fresh lemon juice
2 tablespoons extra-virgin olive oil

Thoroughly combine all the ingredients together in a mixing bowl.

Serving suggestions: With tuna, sea bass, or chicken.

Yield: About 1 cup   **Heat:** 1-2

≈

Chiles have the wonderful quality of bringing all foods to life, which is probably why they are the most widely used seasoning in the world. They're used as such in almost all of the recipes in this book, but in this particular group of salsas, chiles — fresh, dried, and pickled — take center stage.

≈

CHILE
SALSAS

≈ANCHO CHILE SALSA≈

2 ounces (about 5) dried ancho chiles, stemmed and seeded
5 sun-dried tomatoes (not oil-packed)
1 cup brewed coffee, preferably a dark roast such as Guatemalan
3 ounces pitted prunes
2 tablespoons toasted slivered almonds
1 chipotle chile en adobo
1 tablespoon grated Ibarra (Mexican) chocolate, or semi-sweet chocolate
¼ teaspoon toasted ground cumin
1 teaspoon ground canela (1½ teaspoons if using semi-sweet chocolate)

Toast the chiles and rehydrate them in 1 quart of warm water with the sun-dried tomatoes (page 144). Drain the chiles and tomatoes, reserving 1 cup of the water, and transfer to a blender. If it is not bitter, add the reserved chile water; otherwise, add 1 cup of plain water. Add all the remaining ingredients and purée.

Ingredient Note: Ibarra chocolate contains cinnamon and almonds. For availability, see Appendix.

Serving suggestions: With grilled chicken or turkey.

Yield: About 3 cups   **Heat:** 4

≈ CHILE DE ARBOL SALSA ≈

1 ounce dried árbol chiles (about 40), stemmed and seeded
2 Roma tomatoes, blackened
1 teaspoon minced roasted garlic
¼ teaspoon ground toasted cumin
¼ teaspoon ground toasted oregano
¼ teaspoon salt

Toast the chiles and rehydrate them in 1 quart of warm water (page 000) for about 40 minutes. Drain the chiles, reserving 1 cup of the water, and transfer to a food processor or blender. If it is not bitter, add the reserved chile water; otherwise, add 1 cup of plain water. Add the blackened tomatoes, garlic, cumin, oregano, and salt, and purée.

Serving suggestions: With tortilla chips or as a soup garnish.

Yield: About 1½ cups   **Heat:** 9-10

≈ HABANERO SALSA ≈

1 fresh yellow habanero chile, seeded and stemmed
1 yellow tomato, roughly chopped
3 papayas, peeled, seeded, and roughly chopped (about 2 cups)
¾ cup fresh orange juice (about 2 oranges)
2 tablespoons fresh lime juice
1 tablespoon unseasoned rice wine vinegar
1 tablespoon water
1 teaspoon sugar
¼ teaspoon salt

Place all the ingredients in a food processor or blender and purée.

Serving suggestions: With seafood, especially lobster, or grilled chicken.

Yield: About 2½ cups   **Heat:** 6

≈ SALSA BORRACHA ≈

3 ounces dried pasilla chiles (12 to 15), seeded and stemmed
4 tablespoons diced white onion
1½ teaspoons virgin olive oil
1¼ cups (1 bottle) dark beer, such as Negra Modelo
2 cloves roasted garlic
3 Roma tomatoes, blackened
½ teaspoon toasted ground cumin
½ teaspoon toasted ground oregano
¾ teaspoon salt
4 ounces Queso Anejo or feta or dry-aged goat cheese, grated

Toast the chiles and rehydrate them in 2 cups of warm water (page 144). Drain the chiles, reserving ½ cup of the water. Devein the chiles and transfer to a blender. If it is not bitter, add the reserved chile water; otherwise, add ½ cup plain water. Sauté the onion in the oil for 5 minutes over medium heat, and add to the chiles. Add the garlic, tomatoes, cumin, oregano, salt, and beer, and blend until puréed. Transfer to a serving bowl and sprinkle the cheese over the top.

Note: In Spanish, *borracha* means "drunk"; this recipe owes its title to the inclusion of a bottle of beer. True pasilla chiles are dried chilaca chiles. Fresh poblanos are often mistakenly labeled as pasillas, so double-check before buying.

Serving suggestions: With grilled beef or lamb.

Yield: About 3 cups   **Heat:** 4-5

≈ ROASTED GREEN CHILE SALSA ≈

6 to 8 fresh New Mexico green chiles, roasted, peeled, seeded, and diced
2 Roma tomatoes, blackened and roughly chopped
1 teaspoon finely minced fresh oregano
1 heaping teaspoon chopped fresh cilantro
½ teaspoon finely minced fresh marjoram
1 tablespoon La Carreta cilantro apple cider vinegar or other cider vinegar
1 tablespoon extra-virgin olive oil

Thoroughly combine all the ingredients together in a mixing bowl.
Serving suggestions: With tortilla chips, enchiladas, seafood or pork dishes.
Yield: About 2 cups   **Heat:** 3-4

≈ GUAJILLO SALSA ≈

1¼ ounces dried guajillo chiles (about 8), stemmed and seeded
2 tablespoons diced white onion
1 teaspoon virgin olive oil
1 Roma tomato, blackened and roughly chopped
¼ cup toasted pumpkin seeds
1 clove roasted garlic
½ teaspoon salt

Toast the chiles and rehydrate them in 1 quart of warm water (page 144). Drain the chiles, reserving 1 cup of the water, and transfer to a blender. If it is not bitter, add the reserved chile water; otherwise, add 1 cup of plain water. Sauté the onion in the oil for 5 minutes over medium heat and add to the chiles. Add the tomato, pumpkin seeds, garlic, and salt, and purée.
Serving suggestions: With tortilla chips, shrimp, or shellfish.
Yield: About 2 cups   **Heat:** 6

≈ CHIMAYO RED CHILE SALSA ≈

**8 ounces dried Chimayo (New Mexico red) chiles (about 25),
with seeds, stemmed
4 cloves roasted garlic
1 teaspoon salt
1 tablespoon dried oregano, toasted and ground**

Toast the chiles and rehydrate them in 2 quarts of warm water (page 144). Drain the chiles, reserving 2 cups of the water, and transfer to a blender. If it is not bitter, add the reserved chile water; otherwise, add 2 cups of plain water. Add the garlic and salt to the blender and purée. Stir in the oregano.

Serving suggestions: With tortilla chips, enchiladas, grilled or roasted meats, chicken, and grilled shrimp.

Yield: About 3 cups   **Heat:** 5-6

≈ TRICOLOR SALSA ≈

½ cup red bell pepper, seeded and finely diced
½ cup yellow bell pepper, seeded and finely diced
4 teaspoons minced serrano chile, with seeds
⅓ cup La Carreta cilantro apple cider vinegar or other cider vinegar
¼ cup finely chopped fresh cilantro
2 tablespoons minced shallot
2 tablespoons fresh lime juice
1½ teaspoons sugar
¼ teaspoon salt

Thoroughly combine all the ingredients together in a mixing bowl.
Variation: Add ¼ cup finely chopped fresh basil.
Serving Suggestion: With grilled steak, or oysters.
Yield: About 1¼ cups   **Heat:** 6

≈ RAJAS SALSA ≈

1 large red bell pepper, roasted and julienned
1 large yellow bell pepper, roasted and julienned
1 large poblano chile, roasted and julienned
1 Roma tomato, blackened and roughly chopped
4 teaspoons minced fresh cilantro
½ teaspoon chopped roasted garlic
½ teaspoon salt
1 tablespoon extra-virgin olive oil
1 tablespoon fresh lime juice

Thoroughly combine all the ingredients together in a mixing bowl.

Serving suggestions: An all-purpose salsa; and especially good with steak or fish.

Yield: About 2 cups   **Heat:** 2

≈ CHIPOTLE TOMATILLO SALSA ≈

1 pound tomatillos (about 15), blackened and roughly chopped
1 large clove roasted garlic
½ teaspoon sugar
½ teaspoon salt
4 chipotle chiles en adobo
2 tablespoons adobo sauce
⅓ cup chopped fresh cilantro

Place the tomatillos, garlic, sugar, and salt in a food processor or blender. Blend until mostly puréed. Add the chipotles, adobo sauce, and cilantro leaves and blend briefly, leaving the salsa just a little textured.

Variation: Add more chipotles for a more picante salsa.

Serving suggestions: With red meat or pork.

Yield: About 2 cups   **Heat:** 5

≈

Tropical fruits, so luscious and aromatic, are like bottled sunshine. Any one of these salsas will transport you to lands of swaying palms, sun-drenched beaches, and azure seas. These salsas are fragile, so don't expect to hold them for long. Eat, and let your imagination sweep you away.

≈

≈

TROPICAL
S A L S A S

≈

BANANA, TAMARIND, AND MINT SALSA

4 ripe bananas (about 1 pound), peeled and finely diced
¼ cup tamarind paste
2 tablespoons seeded and minced red bell pepper
1 tablespoon minced fresh mint
1 teaspoon brown sugar
1 tablespoon fresh lime juice

Fold all the ingredients together in a mixing bowl.

Note: Tamarind paste has a sweet-tart flavor. It is used in many cuisines, and is available at most Latin, Oriental, and Indian markets.

Serving suggestions: With duck or lamb.

Yield: About 2 cups   **Heat:** 0

≈ AVOCADO-SERRANO SALSA ≈

2 large avocados (about 1 pound), peeled, pitted, and chopped
¼ cup fresh lime juice
1 Roma tomato, diced
3 tablespoons minced red onion
4 teaspoons minced serrano chile, with seeds
2 teaspoons minced fresh cilantro
1½ teaspoons salt

Carefully fold all the ingredients together in a mixing bowl.

Serving suggestions: With tortilla chips, chicken, and as a soup garnish.

Yield: About 2 cups   **Heat:** 4-5

≈ BRAZILIAN AVOCADO AND ORANGE SALSA ≈

1 large avocado, peeled, pitted, and chopped
1 orange, peeled, seeded, and cut into sections
2 tablespoons fresh orange juice
6 tablespoons chopped fresh pineapple
1 Roma tomato, chopped
15 cilantro leaves
1½ teaspoons Coyote Cocina Howlin' Hot Sauce
or other Scotch bonnet chile sauce

Carefully fold all the ingredients together in a mixing bowl.

Serving suggestions: With pork or quail.

Yield: About 2 cups   **Heat:** 3

≈ PAPAYA SALSA ≈

3 papayas, peeled, seeded, and cut into large dice (about 2 cups)
¼ cup fresh lime juice
3 tablespoons shredded dried coconut
2 tablespoons minced fresh cilantro
1 teaspoon Coyote Cocina Howlin' Hot Sauce
or other Scotch bonnet chile sauce
Pinch of sugar

Thoroughly combine all the ingredients together in a mixing bowl.

Serving suggestions: With pork or firm-fleshed fish such as mahi-mahi.

Yield: About 2½ cups   **Heat:** 3

≈ROASTED BANANA SALSA≈

4 ripe bananas (about 1 pound)
1 teaspoon dark rum
1 teaspoon vanilla extract
1 teaspoon maple syrup
½ teaspoon brown sugar
12 macadamia nuts, finely chopped, plus 2 or 3 chopped nuts for garnish

Preheat the oven to 350 degrees. Place the bananas (in their skins) on a cookie sheet or in a baking pan and roast for 30 minutes; the skins will turn dark brown. Let the bananas cool. Peel, dice, and place in a mixing bowl. Add the remaining ingredients and fold together. Sprinkle 2 or 3 more chopped macadamia nuts over the top.

Serving suggestions: With duck or pork.

Yield: About 1¾ cups   **Heat:** 0

≈TROPICAL MANGO SALSA≈

2 mangoes, peeled, pitted, and diced (about 2 cups)
2 teaspoons fresh ginger juice, squeezed in a garlic press
1 tablespoon fresh lime juice
½ teaspoon árbol chile powder or cayenne powder

Thoroughly combine all the ingredients together in a mixing bowl.

Serving suggestions: With tuna or pork.

Yield: About 2¼ cups   **Heat:** 4

≈ SEARED PINEAPPLE SALSA ≈

1 ripe pineapple, peeled, cored, and cut into ¼-inch thick slices
¼ cup red bell pepper, seeded and diced
2 teaspoons chipotle chile purée (page 145)
2 tablespoons fresh orange juice
1 tablespoon fresh lime juice
1 tablespoon finely minced fresh cilantro
2 teaspoons light brown sugar

Cut the pineapple slices in half and dry-sauté in a nonstick pan over medium heat for 8 minutes per side, until caramelized and golden brown. Dice the pineapple and transfer to a mixing bowl. Add the remaining ingredients and combine thoroughly. Taste and add more lime juice or chile purée if desired.

Variation: Peaches may be substituted for the pineapple. Brown until caramelized (peaches will take less time than pineapple).

Serving suggestions: With pork, grilled chicken, or grilled dark-meated, firm-fleshed fish such as tuna, mahi- mahi, or swordfish.

Yield: About 3 cups   **Heat:** 4

≈ HAWAIIAN PINEAPPLE SALSA ≈

2 cups diced fresh pineapple
2 tablespoons minced seeded red bell pepper
2 teaspoons minced serrano chile, with seeds
4 teaspoons minced fresh cilantro
1 teaspoon sugar
1 tablespoon unseasoned rice wine vinegar

Throughly combine all the ingredients together in a mixing bowl.

Serving suggestions: With chicken or pork.

Yield: About 2 cups   **Heat:** 4

≈ MANGO MASH ≈

1 cup diced onion
2 cloves garlic
2 tablespoons grated fresh ginger
3 Roma tomatoes, diced
4 serrano chiles, minced, with seeds
1 cup diced fresh pineapple
1 14-ounce can coconut milk
1 teaspoon achiote paste
1 bunch cilantro, tied
1 mango, peeled, pitted, and diced (about 1 cup)
2 tablespoons chopped fresh cilantro
2 tablespoons fresh lime juice
1 tablespoon Coyote Cocina Howlin' Hot Sauce
or other Scotch bonnet chile sauce

In a saucepan, cook the onion, garlic, ginger, tomatoes, chiles, pineapple, coconut milk, achiote, and bunch of cilantro over medium-high heat, uncovered, for 10 minutes. Remove the cilantro and continue cooking 5 to 10 minutes, until the mixture thickens. Transfer to a blender and purée; there should be about 2 cups of liquid. Refrigerate in the blender jar.

When chilled, remove 1 cup of the liquid (reserve it for another batch of salsa or use it as a soup base or as a pasta sauce with shrimp or scallops). Add the mango, chopped cilantro, lime juice, and hot sauce to the blender and purée.

Note: Achiote paste is brick-red in color and has a distinctive iodine-like flavor. It is available in most Latin or Indian markets.

Serving suggestions: With fish or seafood, especially lobster.

Yield: About 2 cups   **Heat:** 5-6

≈ MELON SALSA ≈

¾ cup diced honeydew melon
¾ cup diced cantaloupe
¾ cup diced watermelon
1½ teaspoons minced serrano chile, with seeds
1½ teaspoons minced fresh mint
1½ teaspoons sugar
1 tablespoon fresh lime juice

Thoroughly combine all the ingredients together in a mixing bowl.

Serving suggestions: With shrimp or chicken.

Yield: About 2¼ cups   **Heat:** 3-4

*Sweet or tart, the natural flavors of fresh
fruits and their color and texture make them
an excellent choice for making great salsas.
It's important to use only those fruits that
are in season and to select the freshest,
best-looking ones you can find. That way you
will be sure of getting maximum flavor and
superior texture. When the selection is poor,
dried fruits are a good alternative, so try
experimenting with those, too.*

≈

FRUIT

SALSAS

≈

≈BALSAMIC BERRY SALSA≈

1 pint strawberries, stemmed and sliced
4 teaspoons balsamic vinegar
1 tablespoon full-bodied red wine (such as a Cabernet or Rhone-style wine)
1 teaspoon sugar
¼ teaspoon freshly ground black pepper

Thoroughly combine all the ingredients together in a mixing bowl.
Serving suggestions: As a summer appetizer, a dessert salsa (with whipped cream or mascarpone), or with pork.
Yield: About 2 cups   **Heat:** 1

≈ORANGE-CHIPOTLE SALSA≈

6 oranges, peeled, seeded, and cut into segments
1 chipotle chile en adobo, thinly julienned
2 tablespoons chipotle chile purée (page 145)
1 teaspoon minced fresh chives

Thoroughly combine all the ingredients together in a mixing bowl.
Serving suggestions: With shellfish, especially clams or mussels.
Yield: About 1¾ cups   **Heat:** 6

≈ CRANBERRY-ORANGE SALSA ≈

2 cups dried cranberries (about 7 ounces)
¾ cup fresh orange juice
1 tablespoon minced orange zest
⅔ cup toasted pecans
4 teaspoons pure red chile powder

Purée all the ingredients together in a food processor or blender.

Serving suggestions: With turkey, quail, or pork.

Yield: About 2 cups   **Heat:** 2-3

≈ CASCABEL-APPLE-RAISIN SALSA ≈

¾ cup raisins
1 cup warm fresh apple cider or water
4 green apples, peeled, cored,
and cut into small dice (about 2 cups)
1 tablespoon sugar
¼ cup fresh apple cider
5 dried cascabel chiles, stemmed and seeded
2 dried pulla chiles, stemmed and seeded
⅛ teaspoon allspice
½ teaspoon canela or cinnamon
Pinch of salt

Slightly rehydrate the raisins in the warm apple cider or water for 5 minutes. Strain, reserving the liquid, and transfer the raisins to a mixing bowl. In a stainless steel saucepan, cook the apples with the sugar and cider for 5 to 7 minutes over medium heat until tender. Stir in the raisins.

Toast the cascabel and pulla chiles and rehydrate them in ⅔ cup of the reserved raisin liquid (page 144). Drain the chiles, again reserving the liquid, and transfer to a food processor or blender. If it is not bitter, add the reserved liquid; otherwise, add ⅔ cup plain water. Add 2 tablespoons of the apple-raisin mixture and purée. Transfer to a saucepan and reduce by about half over medium-high heat; the mixture will be quite thick. Sieve through a fine strainer into a clean bowl, discarding the solids.

Add the rest of the apple-raisin mixture, the allspice, canela or cinnamon, and salt, and combine thoroughly.

Serving suggestions: With pork or duck.

Yield: About 2 cups   **Heat:** 4-5

≈ PEAR AND BLACK OLIVE SALSA ≈

1 tablespoon canola oil
3 pears, peeled, cored, and diced
1 teaspoon sugar
8 Niçoise or Kalamata olives, pitted and sliced
3 Roma tomatoes, oven-roasted and diced
1 small poblano chile, roasted, peeled, seeded, and diced
1 small red bell pepper (or 1 fresh New Mexico red chile), roasted,
peeled, seeded, and diced
1 tablespoon La Carreta cilantro apple cider vinegar or
other cider vinegar

Heat the oil in a pan and sauté the pear with the sugar over medium-low heat for 2 minutes. Transfer to a mixing bowl. Thoroughly combine with the remaining ingredients.

Serving suggestions: With turkey or quail.

Yield: About 2 cups   **Heat:** 3-4

≈ MOROCCAN DATE SALSA ≈

8 ounces pitted dates (about 10), cut in half
2 cups water
¼ cup fresh orange juice
2 tablespoons fresh lemon juice
1 tablespoon minced lemon zest
1 tablespoon honey
1 tablespoon sherry vinegar
1½ teaspoons freshly ground black pepper
½ teaspoon ground cinnamon
½ teaspoon ground canela or
¼ teaspoon additional ground cinnamon
¼ teaspoon ground cumin
½ teaspoon cayenne powder
⅛ teaspoon ground allspice
1 tablespoon chopped fresh cilantro
2 tablespoons chopped fresh mint

Cook the dates in the water over medium-high heat for 8 to 10 minutes until soft and the water has reduced to 1 cup. Transfer to a food processor or blender, add all the remaining ingredients, and purée.

Note: If canela is unavailable, use ¼ teaspoon more cinnamon.

Serving suggestions: With lamb, chicken, fish, or as a sandwich spread.

Yield: About 1½ cups   **Heat:** 4

≈ APPLE-PASADO SALSA ≈

6 dried New Mexico green chiles (chile pasado),
stemmed and ground, with seeds (about ¼ cup)
2 cups fresh apple cider
6 Granny Smith apples, peeled, cored, and sliced (about 3 cups)
¼ cup piñons (pine nuts), toasted
1 tablespoon pure maple syrup

Heat the cider in a saucepan, add the ground green chiles, and over high heat, reduce the liquid by half. Lower the heat to medium-high, add the apples, and cook until tender, about 10 minutes. Transfer to a food processor or blender, add the pine nuts and maple syrup, and pulse together; the mixture should be a little chunky.

Serving suggestions: With pork or duck.

Yield: About 2½ cups   **Heat:** 6-7

≈ LEMON-FIG SALSA ≈

2 cups dried figs (about 20)
Zest of 1½ lemons, finely minced
2 tablespoons minced fresh Italian parsley
2 teaspoons minced fresh thyme leaves
½ teaspoon cayenne powder
2 teaspoons pure lemon extract
¾ cup extra-virgin olive oil

Purée all the ingredients together in a food processor or blender.

Variation: Substitute ¾ cup pure lemon oil for olive oil and lemon extract.

Serving suggestions: With grilled fish, or on pasta.

Yield: About 1¼ cups   **Heat:** 2-3

≈ APPLE AND GREEN CHILE ≈ SALSA

1 cup fresh apple cider
2 green apples, peeled, cored, and diced
4 tablespoons diced onion
1½ teaspoons virgin olive oil
2 fresh New Mexico green chiles,
roasted, peeled, seeded, and diced
½ teaspoon toasted oregano,
rubbed between the fingers
1 teaspoon sugar
1 teaspoon fresh lemon juice
1 teaspoon balsamic vinegar

In a saucepan over high heat, reduce the apple cider down to ½ cup. Lower the heat to medium, add the diced apple, and cook for 5 minutes until soft. Transfer to a mixing bowl. In a skillet, sauté the onion in the oil for 5 minutes. Add to the bowl, along with the remaining ingredients, and combine thoroughly.

Serving suggestions: As a side with grilled chicken or pork.

Yield: About 2½ cups   **Heat:** 2-3

≈ GRAPEFRUIT-PERSIMMON ≈ SALSA

4 grapefruit, about 1 pound each, peeled, seeded, and cut into sections
½ cup fresh grapefruit juice
2 fully ripe persimmons, tops sliced off, halved, and cored
1 teaspoon sugar
1 teaspoon minced fresh cilantro leaves
1 teaspoon Coyote Cocina Howlin' Hot Sauce
or other Scotch bonnet chile sauce
1 tablespoon fresh lime juice

Place the grapefruit sections and juice in a mixing bowl. Cut the persimmon halves into sections the same size as the grapefruit sections, and add to the bowl. Thoroughly combine with the sugar, cilantro, chile sauce, and lime juice. Garnish with a few whole cilantro leaves.

Variation: Add ¼ teaspoon finely ground canela or ground cinnamon.

Note: Persimmons are usually in season in late fall through February. Only use ripe persimmons that are soft to the touch; otherwise they (and the salsa) will taste bitter.

Serving suggestions: With tuna, swordfish, or pork.

Yield: About 2½ cups   **Heat:** 4

Corn is native to the Americas, and was one of the four "magic plants" that sustained pre-Columbian civilizations (the others being chiles, beans, and squash). Corn should be used as fresh as possible; peak season is May through September. A number of the following recipes call for roasting corn, which gives it additional flavor dimensions and a rich earthiness that I particularly like.

≈

≈

CORN

SALSAS

≈

≈CORN AND SQUASH SALSA≈

2 tablespoons diced onion
¼ cup water
2 ears corn
**1½ cups yellow crookneck squash or yellow zucchini,
diced to the size of corn kernels**
1 tablespoon unsalted butter
**2 large sprigs fresh marjoram,
plus 2 sprigs for garnish**
**5 Roma tomatoes, oven-roasted and diced,
or ¼ cup sun-dried tomatoes (in oil), drained and diced**
1 teaspoon minced fresh marjoram
⅓ teaspoon salt

In a sauté pan, cook the onion and water together over low heat, covered, for 10 minutes. Cut the corn kernels from the cobs with a sharp knife (about 1½ cups). Add to the sauté pan together with squash, butter, and 2 sprigs marjoram. Cook for 5 minutes longer, until the vegetables are soft and the liquid has evaporated. Discard the marjoram and transfer to a mixing bowl.

Add the tomatoes, marjoram, and salt and thoroughly combine. Chill before serving. Garnish with 2 fresh marjoram sprigs.

Serving suggestions: With eggs or as a brunch side dish.

Yield: About 2¼ cups   **Heat:** 0

≈ CORN, GREENS, AND ≈
BACON SALSA

8 strips bacon
3 ears corn
¼ cup water
**3 tablespoons La Carreta chile apple cider vinegar
or other cider vinegar**
**8 ounces mixed watercress, mustard greens, and arugula,
roughly julienned**
2 red Thai or red serrano chiles, thinly sliced, with seeds
2 tablespoons extra-virgin olive oil
¼ teaspoon salt
½ teaspoon freshly ground black pepper

Cook the bacon in a sauté pan or skillet until done but not crisp, and dice. Transfer to a mixing bowl.

Cut the corn kernels from the cobs with a sharp knife (about 2 cups). Place in a sauté pan with the water, and cook for 2 to 3 minutes over medium heat until tender and the water has just evaporated. Add to the mixing bowl.

Heat the vinegar in a large pan or skillet and wilt the greens over medium heat for 30 seconds. Add to the mixing bowl along with the chiles, oil, salt, and pepper, and thoroughly combine.

Serving suggestions: With pork or eggs.

Yield: About 2 cups   **Heat:** 5-6

≈ CORN AND RAJAS SALSA ≈

3 ears corn
¼ cup water
1 tablespoon peanut oil
½ cup julienned white onion
5 fresh red Fresno or red jalapeño chiles, roasted,
peeled, seeded, and julienned
5 fresh green jalapeño chiles, roasted, peeled, seeded, and julienned
1 cup fresh cilantro leaves, loosely packed
1 tablespoon fresh lime juice
½ teaspoon ground toasted coriander seed
¼ teaspoon salt

Cut the corn kernels from the cobs with a sharp knife (about 2 cups). Place in a sauté pan with the water, and cook for 2 to 3 minutes over medium heat until tender and the water has just evaporated. Transfer to a mixing bowl.

Heat the oil in a sauté pan and sauté the onion over medium heat for about 8 minutes or until slightly brown. Transfer to the mixing bowl, add the roasted chiles and remaining ingredients, and thoroughly combine.

Serving suggestions: With grilled chicken or on the side with barbecued foods.

Yield: About 2¼ cups   **Heat:** 8

≈ CORN AND JERKY SALSA ≈

3 ears corn
1 ounce beef or venison jerky, diced (about ⅓ cup)
⅓ cup warm water
1½ teaspoons olive oil
4 tablespoons diced white onion
1 dried New Mexico green chile (chile pasado),
stemmed and ground with seeds
1 tablespoon truffle oil (or wild mushroom oil)
1 clove roasted garlic, minced
¼ teaspoon salt

Cut the corn kernels from the cobs with a sharp knife (about 2 cups). Heat a large, heavy-bottomed sauté pan or skillet over high heat until almost smoking. Place no more than two layers of the corn kernels in the pan at a time, and dry-roast for 4 to 5 minutes until smoky and dark, tossing continuously.

Rehydrate the jerky in the water for 2 minutes or until softened. Pat dry with paper towels, and reserve 3 tablespoons of the water.

Heat the oil in a sauté pan and sauté the onion over medium heat for 5 minutes or until translucent. Transfer to a mixing bowl. Add the corn, jerky, reserved jerky water, and the remaining ingredients, and thoroughly combine.

Serving suggestions: With chicken or eggs.

Yield: About 2 cups   **Heat:** 3-4

≈ CORN AND BEAN SALSA ≈

5 ounces dried pinto beans
2 to 3 cups water
3 ears corn
Pinch of salt
¼ teaspoon sugar
2 Roma tomatoes, diced
½ cup mixed pickled vegetables
(onions, carrots, and hot chiles), diced
2 tablespoons pickling liquid
2 tablespoons extra-virgin olive oil
¼ teaspoon salt

Place the pinto beans in a saucepan with enough water to cover by at least 1½ inches. Bring the water to a boil, reduce the heat to a simmer, and cook uncovered for about 40 minutes or until tender. Add more water if necessary to keep the beans covered. Drain and allow to cool (there should be about 1 cup of cooked beans).

Cut the corn kernels from the cobs with a sharp knife (about 2 cups). Place in a sauté pan with ¼ cup of water, salt, and sugar, and cook for 2 minutes over high heat. Transfer to a mixing bowl. Add the beans and the remaining ingredients, and thoroughly combine.

Note: Pickled vegetables can be purchased at most specialty markets, or buy vegetables "en escabeche" at a Latin market. Remove any herbs or peppercorns before using the vegetables for this recipe.

Serving suggestions: With eggs, chicken, or as a side dish.

Yield: About 2¾ cups   **Heat:** 3-4

〰〰〰〰〰

≈ ROASTED CORN AND
WILD MUSHROOM SALSA ≈

4 ears fresh corn

⅓ cup cleaned and diced morels or other wild mushrooms

3 teaspoons extra-virgin olive oil

¼ cup sun-dried tomatoes (in oil), finely diced,
with 1 teaspoon of their oil

2 poblano chiles, roasted, peeled, seeded, and diced

2 teaspoons minced fresh marjoram

1 clove roasted garlic, minced

1 teaspoon adobo sauce

1 teaspoon fresh lime juice

½ teaspoon sherry vinegar

½ teaspoon salt

Cut the corn kernels from the cobs with a sharp knife (about 3 cups). Heat a large, heavy-bottomed sauté pan or skillet over high heat until almost smoking. Place no more than two layers of the corn kernels in the pan at a time, and dry-roast for 4 to 5 minutes until smoky and dark, tossing continuously.

Sauté the mushrooms in ½ teaspoon of the olive oil until they are cooked well, about 10 minutes. Transfer to a mixing bowl, add the corn, remaining olive oil, and the rest of the ingredients, and thoroughly combine.

Note: If fresh wild mushrooms aren't available, use a combination of dried wild and fresh domestic mushrooms.

Serving suggestions: This is a very versatile salsa; especially good with chicken, grilled steak, or as a side dish.

Yield: About 3 cups   **Heat:** 4-5

〰〰〰〰〰

≈ CORN AND HUITLACOCHE ≈ SALSA

4 serrano chiles, roasted, peeled, and chopped, with seeds
5 Roma tomatoes, diced
2 cups huitlacoche (about 11 ounces)
¼ cup huitlacoche liquid (see note below)
½ cup minced white onion
4 cloves roasted garlic, mashed
1 teaspoon minced fresh epazote
12 cilantro leaves
½ teaspoon salt
1 ear corn
2 tablespoons water
1 teaspoon adobo sauce

Place the serranos, tomatoes, huitlacoche, huitlacoche liquid, onion, garlic, epazote, cilantro, and salt in a sauté pan or skillet, and sauté over medium heat for 20 minutes. Transfer to a mixing bowl.

Cut the corn kernels from the cob with a sharp knife (about ¾ cup). Place in a pan with the water and adobo sauce, and cook over medium heat for 2 minutes. Fold into the ingredients in the mixing bowl.

Note: Huitlacoche, "the Mexican truffle," is a fungus that grows on corn and is considered a delicacy in Mexico. It is available frozen (see Appendix for sources); the liquid referred to in this recipe is yielded when the huitlacoche is defrosted.

Serving suggestions: With beef or pork.

Yield: About 2 cups   **Heat:** 5

≈ CORN AND GINGER SALSA ≈

3 ears corn
2 tablespoons water
2 tablespoons fresh ginger juice, squeezed in a garlic press
1½ tablespoons peanut oil
Pinch of sugar
Pinch of salt
¼ teaspoon ground coriander seed
1 red bell pepper, roasted, peeled, seeded, and finely diced
2 dried árbol chiles, crumbled
3 tablespoons fresh orange juice
¼ teaspoon cinnamon
Pinch of saffron (about 4 threads)

Cut the corn kernels from the cobs with a sharp knife (about 2 cups). Place in a saucepan with the water, ginger juice, oil, sugar, salt, and coriander. Cook over medium-high heat for 2 minutes. Remove from the heat and transfer to a mixing bowl. Add the remaining ingredients and thoroughly combine.

Variation: Add 1 tablespoon minced fresh basil.

Serving suggestions: With grilled lamb or duck.

Yield: About 2 cups   **Heat:** 4

≈ CORN AND GREEN CHILE SALSA ≈

3 ears corn
¼ cup water
1½ teaspoons olive oil
4 tablespoons diced onion
1 pound fresh New Mexico green chiles (8 to 10),
roasted, peeled, seeded, and finely diced
5 Roma tomatoes, oven-roasted and finely diced
3 tablespoons La Carreta apple cider vinegar
or other cider vinegar
½ teaspoon sugar
¼ teaspoon salt
¼ teaspoon toasted oregano, rubbed between the fingers

Cut the corn kernels from the cobs with a sharp knife (about 2 cups).
Place in a sauté pan with the water, and cook for 2 to 3 minutes over
medium heat until tender and the water has just evaporated. Transfer to a mixing bowl.

Heat the oil in a sauté pan and sauté the onion over medium heat
for about 5 minutes, or until translucent. Add to the mixing bowl
along with the remaining ingredients, and thoroughly combine.

Serving suggestions: With chicken, or as a soup garnish.

Yield: About 2¼ cups   **Heat:** 4-5

≈ RANCHO CORN SALSA ≈

2 dried New Mexico red chiles, stemmed and seeded
3 ears corn
1½ teaspoons virgin olive oil
4 tablespoons finely diced onion
2 Roma tomatoes, blackened and chopped
1 clove roasted garlic, mashed
½ teaspoon salt
½ teaspoon toasted ground cumin
½ teaspoon toasted oregano, rubbed between the fingers
1 tablespoon fresh lime juice

Toast the chiles and rehydrate them in 1 cup of warm water (page 144). Drain the chiles and julienne in short strips.

Cut the corn kernels from the cobs with a sharp knife (about 2 cups). Heat a large, heavy-bottomed sauté pan or skillet over high heat until almost smoking. Place no more than two layers of the corn kernels in the pan at a time, and dry-roast for 4 to 5 minutes until smoky and dark, tossing continuously.

Heat the oil in a sauté pan over medium heat, add the onion, and sauté for about 5 minutes or until translucent. Transfer to a mixing bowl, add the julienned chiles, roasted corn, and remaining ingredients, and thoroughly combine.

Serving suggestions: With chicken or eggs.

Yield: About 2 cups

Heat: 5

≈

Another of the staples of the pre-Columbian New World, cooked, dried beans are a wonderful medium for carrying soft, subtle flavors. Beans are also highly nutritious — they are rich in protein, iron, phosphorous and calcium — and their healthfulness makes them an important part of any vegetarian diet.

≈

BEAN
SALSAS

≈ SWEET 'N' HOT BEAN SALSA ≈

½ cup dried black beans, washed
⅔ teaspoon salt
**2 fresh habanero chiles, sliced into rings, with seeds,
or 2 tablespoons Coyote Cocina Howlin' Hot Sauce**
**½ cup ginger juice (about 8 ounces fresh ginger root, grated
and squeezed in a garlic press)**
¾ cup sugar
¼ cup water
2 yellow tomatoes, seeded and diced
1 tablespoon fresh lime juice

Cook the beans for 1 to 1½ hours, or until just tender, adding ⅓ teaspoon of the salt towards the end (see page 144). Drain the beans and transfer to a clean pan.

Add the habaneros, ginger juice, sugar, and ¼ cup water to the beans, and bring to a boil. Reduce the heat, cover, and simmer for 15 minutes. Remove from the heat and strain off the liquid (this can be used as a barbecue glaze for grilled chicken or pork). Lightly rinse the beans and habanero mixture under running water and transfer to a mixing bowl. Add the tomatoes, lime juice, and the remaining ⅓ teaspoon salt, and thoroughly combine.
Serving suggestions: With fish or shellfish.
Yield: About 1¾ cups   **Heat:** 7

≈ PINTO THREE CHILE SALSA ≈

¾ cup dried pinto beans, washed
1 teaspoon salt
3 dried árbol chiles, with seeds
3 dried pasilla chiles, seeded
2 dried or canned chipotle chiles
2 strips bacon, diced
1 tablespoon virgin olive oil
⅓ white onion, diced
2 cloves roasted garlic
2 Roma tomatoes, blackened
¾ cup dark beer
1 tablespoon peanut oil
1 teaspoon cider vinegar
2 jalapeño chiles, roasted, peeled, seeded, and diced, for garnish

Cook the beans for 1½ to 2 hours, or until tender, adding ½ teaspoon salt towards the end (see page 144). Drain the beans and transfer to a mixing bowl.

Toast the arbol and pasilla chiles together and rehydrate with the dried chipotle chiles in 1 cup of warm water. If using canned chipotles, there is no need to rehydrate them. Drain and set aside.

Sauté the bacon over medium heat for about 5 minutes, until just cooked and still soft. Set aside. Heat the oil in a sauté pan or skillet and sauté the onion for about 10 minutes over medium-high heat, until browned and caramelized. Transfer to a blender, add the rehydrated chiles, canned chipotle if used, garlic, tomatoes, beer, and remaining ½ teaspoon salt, and purée.

In a heavy pan or skillet, heat the peanut oil until just smoking. Add the puréed mixture and refry, uncovered, for 5 to 8 minutes over high heat until reduced and thickened. Transfer ¾ cup of the sauce to the mixing bowl, add the cider vinegar and

(continued on page 82)

reserved bacon, and combine with the beans. Garnish with the diced jalapeño sprinkled over the top.

Note: Any leftover refried sauce can be served as a dipping sauce.

Serving suggestions: With steak or grilled meats.

Yield: About 2 cups   **Heat:** 7

COWBOY CAVIAR
≈ (BLACK-EYED PEA SALSA) ≈

³⁄₄ cup black-eyed peas, washed
2 green jalapeño chiles, halved
3 teaspoons salt
3 or 4 sprigs each marjoram and thyme
1 cup cider vinegar
1 stick canela or cinnamon
2 cups water
8 black peppercorns
2 bay leaves
¼ bunch fresh cilantro, tied
1 fresh New Mexico red chile, 1 red jalapeño,
1 green jalapeño, seeded and cut into fine rings
1 small red bell pepper, seeded and diced
½ cup each diced celery and carrots
1 small red onion, cut into fine rings
3 green serrano chiles, sliced into rings
1 yellow tomato, diced
2 tablespoons extra-virgin olive oil
¼ cup finely sliced scallion (green part only), for garnish

Cook the black-eyed peas and halved jalapeños for about 45 minutes to 1 hour, or until the beans are tender, adding ½ teaspoon salt towards the end (see page 144). Drain and transfer to a mixing bowl.

Tie the marjoram and thyme sprigs together. Place in a large stainless steel pan with the vinegar, 2 teaspoons salt, canela or cinnamon, water, peppercorns, and bay leaves. Bring to a boil, reduce the heat, and simmer for 15 minutes. Add the cilantro and simmer for 5 minutes longer. Strain, discarding the solids, and return the liquid to the pan.

Add the New Mexico chiles, red and green jalapeño rings, bell pepper, celery, and carrot, and simmer until the vegetables are just al dente, about 5 minutes. Add the onion rings and simmer for 2 minutes longer. Strain the liquid and return to the pan, and transfer the vegetables to the mixing bowl with the beans.

Heat the strained cooking liquid, add the serranos, and reduce over high heat to about 3 tablespoons of liquid. Transfer all to the mixing bowl. Add the tomato, oil, and remaining ½ teaspoon salt. Garnish with the sliced scallion sprinkled over the top.

Serving suggestions: With ham or eggs.

Yield: About 2½ cups   **Heat:** 5

≈ MIXED BEAN SALSA ≈

2 tablespoons each dried black beans, Anasazi beans,
black-eyed peas, Flor de Mayo red beans, pinto beans,
and scarlet runner beans, washed

¾ teaspoon salt

3 tablespoons extra-virgin olive oil

½ eggplant diced, with peel (about 1 cup)

Pinch of freshly ground black pepper

½ clove garlic, minced

3 fresh New Mexico green chiles, roasted, peeled, seeded, and diced

⅓ cup roasted red bell pepper, peeled, seeded, and diced

5 Roma tomatoes, oven-roasted and diced

¼ cup peeled and diced cucumber

2 tablespoons minced fresh mint plus 1 tablespoon chopped
fresh mint, for garnish

2 tablespoons finely minced lemon zest

2½ tablespoons fresh lemon juice

Cook the beans for 1 to 1½ hours, or until tender, adding ½ teaspoon salt towards the end (see page 144). Drain the beans.

Season the eggplant with the remaining ¼ teaspoon salt and
the pepper. Heat 2 tablespoons of the olive oil in a sauté pan and
sauté the eggplant with the garlic for 4 to 5 minutes or until light
brown. Transfer to a mixing bowl, add the beans, the remaining 1
tablespoon olive oil, and the rest of the ingredients, and thoroughly
combine. Garnish with 1 tablespoon chopped fresh mint.

Note: Substitute other beans, as long as you get a mix of colors.
You need about ¾ cup total.

Serving suggestions: With grilled poultry.

Yield: About 3¼ cups   **Heat:** 4-5

≈ ANASAZI BEAN SALSA ≈

½ cup dried Anasazi beans or red beans, washed

2 fresh epazote leaves plus 1 teaspoon minced fresh epazote

⅔ teaspoon salt

2 dried guajillo chiles

3 tablespoons virgin olive oil

4 cups diced wild mushrooms, such as chanterelles,
portobellos or shiitakes, or domestic mushrooms

2 teaspoons minced garlic

¼ teaspoon freshly ground black pepper

2 Roma tomatoes, blackened

Cook the beans with the epazote leaves for 45 minutes to 1 hour,
or until tender, adding ⅓ teaspoon salt towards the end (see page
144). Remove the epazote leaves, drain the beans, and transfer to
a mixing bowl.

Toast the guajillos and rehydrate them in 1 cup warm water. Drain
the chiles, finely julienne, and add to the mixing bowl.

Heat the olive oil in a sauté pan or skillet and sauté the mushrooms, garlic, remaining ⅓ teaspoon salt, and pepper over
medium-high heat for about 5 minutes, until tender. Transfer to the
mixing bowl. Cut the blackened tomatoes in half and squeeze out
and discard the seeds and juice. Dice the pulp, add it to the mixing
bowl along with the minced epazote, and gently combine all.

Serving suggestions: With antelope, venison or beef.

Yield: About 2¼ cups   **Heat:** 4

FLOR DE MAYO
RED BEAN SALSA

¾ cup dried Flor de Mayo red beans,
or other variety of red bean, washed

1 teaspoon salt

1 teaspoon virgin olive oil

2 tablespoons diced white onion

3 Roma tomatoes, blackened

5 dried árbol chiles, ground, with seeds

1 clove garlic

1½ tablespoons honey

2 tablespoons La Carreta chile apple cider vinegar
or other cider vinegar

2 tablespoons water

1 teaspoon butter

¾ cup diced fresh pineapple

2 ounces ham, finely diced (about ½ cup)

2 teaspoons peanut oil

¼ cup sliced scallions, for garnish

Cook the beans for about 45 minutes to 1 hour, or until tender, adding ½ teaspoon salt towards the end (see page 144). Drain the beans and set aside.

Heat the oil in a pan and sauté the onion over medium heat for 5 minutes or until translucent. Transfer to a food processor and add the tomatoes, ground chiles, garlic, honey, vinegar, water, and remaining ½ teaspoon salt. Purée and set aside.

Melt the butter in a sauté pan or skillet and sauté the pineapple for 5 minutes over medium heat until tender. Stir in the ham, warm through, and remove from heat.

In a separate large pan or skillet, heat the peanut oil until just smoking. Add the puréed mixture and refry for 30 seconds over high heat. Transfer to a mixing bowl, add the pineapple and ham, and fold in the beans. Let cool, and garnish with scallions.

Serving suggestions: As a side for brunch or as a picnic dish.

Yield: About 3½ cups   **Heat:** 6

MEDITERRANEAN
WHITE BEAN SALSA

¾ cup dried white pea beans, washed

½ teaspoon salt

½ cup sun-dried tomatoes (in oil), drained and diced

1 tablespoon minced anchovy

2 tablespoons sliced pitted Niçoise or Kalamata olives

2 teaspoons finely minced lemon zest

2 tablespoons minced fresh Italian parsley

¾ teaspoon cayenne powder

2 tablespoons extra-virgin olive oil

2 tablespoons fresh lemon juice

Cook the beans for 45 minutes to 1 hour, or until tender, adding the salt towards the end (see page 144). Drain the beans, allow to cool, and transfer to a mixing bowl. Add the remaining ingredients to the mixing bowl and thoroughly combine.

Serving suggestions: With grilled tuna or sea bass.

Yield: About 3½ cups   **Heat:** 5

~~~~~~~~~

≈ MARK'S BLACK BEAN SALSA ≈

$^3/_4$ cup dried black beans, washed
1 teaspoon salt
1 red bell pepper, roasted, seeded, peeled, and diced
1 yellow bell pepper, roasted, seeded, peeled, and diced
2 chipotle chiles en adobo, minced
2 teaspoons finely minced orange zest
$^1/_2$ teaspoon minced fresh marjoram
1 teaspoon minced fresh cilantro
2 tablespoons sherry vinegar
2 tablespoons extra-virgin olive oil

Cook the beans for 1 to $1^1/_2$ hours, or until tender, adding $^1/_2$ teaspoon salt towards the end (see page 144). Drain the beans, allow to cool, and transfer to a mixing bowl.

Add the remaining $^1/_2$ teaspoon salt and the rest of the ingredients, and thoroughly combine.

Variation: Add 6 strips bacon, sautéed and diced (about 3 tablespoons).

Serving suggestions: With beef or a meaty fish like swordfish or tuna.

Yield: About $2^1/_2$ cups   **Heat:** 2-3

~~~~~~~~~

≈ BARBADOS BLACK BEAN SALSA ≈

$^1/_2$ cup dried black beans, washed
$^1/_3$ teaspoon salt
1 cup diced mango (2 small mangoes)
3 tablespoons seeded and finely diced red bell pepper
1 tablespoon Coyote Cocina Howlin' Hot Sauce
or other Scotch bonnet chile sauce
1 tablespoon fresh lime juice

Cook the beans for 1 to $1^1/_2$ hours, or until tender, adding $^1/_2$ teaspoon salt towards the end (see page 144). Drain the beans and let cool. Transfer to a mixing bowl, add the remaining ingredients, and fold together.

Serving suggestions: With grilled lobster or fish such as snapper.

Yield: About $2^1/_4$ cups   **Heat:** 5-6

~~~~~~~~~

AZTEC WHITE BEAN, LEEK, AND MUSHROOM SALSA

½ cup white Aztec beans
or large white beans, washed
⅔ teaspoon salt
1 large leek, sliced in rings
(white part and 2 slices of the green)
1 teaspoon extra-virgin olive oil
3 ounces portobello mushroom,
or domestic mushrooms, sliced
⅛ teaspoon minced garlic
½ red bell pepper, roasted, seeded, peeled,
and cut into strips
1 fresh New Mexico green chile, roasted, seeded, peeled,
and cut into strips
¾ teaspoon fresh thyme
½ teaspoon fresh lemon juice
1 red Fresno chile, cut into thin rings, for garnish

Cook the beans for 1 to 1½ hours, or until tender, adding ⅓ teaspoon salt towards the end (see page 144).

Blanch the leek rings in ¼ cup boiling water for 2 minutes, and drain. Heat the olive oil in a large sauté pan or skillet and sauté the leeks, mushrooms, and garlic for 2 minutes over high heat. Transfer to the mixing bowl. Add the bell pepper and green chile strips, thyme, lemon juice, and remaining ⅓ teaspoon salt, and combine. Garnish with the red Fresno chile rings sprinkled over the top.

Serving suggestions: With pork or ham dishes.

Yield: About 2½ cups   **Heat:** 3-4

≈

Here's a great way to use the summer bounty from your vegetable garden. Vegetables provide texture and crunch as well as color and flavor to salsas. They are a great creative alternative to the humdrum vegetable side dish.

≈

GARDEN
SALSAS

≈ ARTICHOKE-APPLE SALSA ≈

4 quarts water
Juice of 4 lemons
1 teaspoon salt
10 baby artichokes
1½ teaspoons peanut oil
2 green apples, peeled, cored, and diced
1 teaspoon sugar
3 Roma tomatoes, blackened and diced
¼ cup diced poblano chile, roasted, peeled, and seeded
1 tablespoon minced fresh mint
1 tablespoon extra-virgin olive oil
¼ teaspoon salt

Bring the water, lemon juice and salt to a boil in a large stockpot. Submerge the artichokes with a weight and cook for about 20 minutes or until tender at the base. Remove the cooked artichokes and let cool. Peel off and discard the hard leaves, exposing the soft leaves and the choke. Cut into quarters (there should be about 1 cup); transfer to a mixing bowl.

Heat the peanut oil in a sauté pan and sauté the apples with the sugar over medium-high heat for about 5 minutes, or until soft but still firm. Add to the mixing bowl, together with remaining ingredients, and combine thoroughly.

Serving suggestions: With chicken or pork.

Yield: About 2¼ cups   **Heat:** 3

≈ EGGPLANT-CHIPOTLE SALSA ≈

¼ cup peanut oil
1 eggplant (about 1½ pounds), peeled and finely diced
(about 4 cups)
4 cloves garlic, minced
¾ teaspoon salt
5 ounces small green beans (haricots verts),
sliced into 1-inch lengths
4 chipotle chiles en adobo, julienned
1 teaspoon adobo sauce
2 tablespoons roasted, peeled, seeded,
and finely diced red bell pepper
1 tablespoon sherry vinegar

Heat the oil in a large skillet and sauté the eggplant, garlic and salt over medium heat for 3 to 4 minutes. Transfer to a mixing bowl.

Blanch the beans in boiling salted water for 30 seconds, drain, and add to the mixing bowl along with the remaining ingredients, and thoroughly combine.

Serving suggestions: With lamb or chicken.

Yield: About 2½ cups   **Heat:** 7-8

≈GRILLED VEGETABLE SALSA≈

1 fresh New Mexico green chile, seeded and halved
1 red bell pepper, seeded and halved
1 small Japanese eggplant, halved
1 zucchini, halved
2 ounces wild mushrooms, such as shiitakes,
chanterelles, or morels
4 spears asparagus
4 tablespoons extra-virgin olive oil
Salt and freshly ground black pepper to taste
2 tablespoons balsamic vinegar
1½ teaspoons chopped fresh marjoram
½ teaspoon salt
Pinch cayenne powder

Brush the chile, bell pepper, eggplant, zucchini, wild mushrooms, and asparagus with 2 tablespoons olive oil and season with salt and pepper. Grill the vegetables until done, let cool, and dice. Transfer to a mixing bowl. Add the remaining 2 tablespoons olive oil, balsamic vinegar, marjoram, salt, and cayenne, and thoroughly combine.

Serving suggestions: With grilled meats, rice, or pasta.

Yield: About 2 cups   **Heat:** 2

≈ CABBAGE SALSA ≈

1½ cups unseasoned rice wine vinegar
1 cup water
4 serrano chiles, cut into rings
3 tablespoons sugar
½ teaspoon salt
8 ounces cabbage, tough outer leaves and stem removed,
diced (about 2 packed cups)
1½ cups peeled, cored, and finely diced pineapple
3 tablespoons seeded and diced red bell pepper
1 tablespoon minced fresh cilantro

Put the vinegar, water, serranos, sugar, and salt in a large saucepan, and bring to a boil. Reduce the liquid by half, about 10 minutes. Add the cabbage and cook for 1 minute, stirring occasionally. Strain, reserving the liquid, and cool the cabbage in a bowl placed over a larger bowl of ice water.

When cool, add 1 tablespoon of the reserved cooking liquid, the pineapple, bell pepper, and cilantro. Thoroughly combine.

Serving suggestions: With barbecued food, especially ribs.

Yield: About 2 cups   **Heat:** 5

≈ SWEET POTATO PECAN SALSA ≈

½ teaspoon sugar
½ teaspoon salt
1½ pounds sweet potatoes, peeled and diced (about 3 cups)
¼ cup toasted pecans
¼ cup dried cranberries
¼ cup pure maple syrup
1 tablespoon pure red chile powder
¼ cup water
2 tablespoons fresh orange juice

Bring a large pot of water to a boil, add the sugar and salt, and blanch the sweet potatoes for 4 minutes. Drain the sweet potatoes in a sieve or strainer, and shock them under cold running water. Transfer to a mixing bowl, and add the pecans.

Rehydrate the cranberries in enough hot water to cover for 5 minutes. Drain and add to the mixing bowl.

In a saucepan, cook the maple syrup, chile powder, and ¼ cup water together for about 4 minutes over medium heat or until the liquid is reduced by half. Let cool, add to the mixing bowl with the orange juice, and thoroughly combine.

Serving suggestions: With turkey, ham, or squab.

Yield: About 3 cups   **Heat:** 3

≈ CREOLE SALSA ≈

1 small red bell pepper, peeled, seeded and diced
1 stalk celery, diced
2 red Fresno chiles or green jalapeños,
minced, with seeds
1 large clove garlic, minced
1 bay leaf
1 sprig fresh thyme
Pinch of salt
4 teaspoons Tabasco® sauce
¾ cup water
¼ cup virgin olive oil
8 ounces eggplant, peeled and diced (about 1½ cups)
5 Roma tomatoes, oven-roasted and diced
3 scallions, green ends removed,
sliced lengthwise
1 teaspoon minced fresh thyme
1 tablespoon extra-virgin olive oil

Place the bell pepper, celery, chiles, garlic, herbs, salt, Tabasco and water in a saucepan and cook, uncovered, over medium-high heat for about 10 minutes, or until the water evaporates. Remove from the heat, discard the bay leaf and thyme, transfer to a mixing bowl, and allow to cool.

Heat the ¼ cup virgin olive oil in a large skillet and sauté the eggplant over medium heat until tender, about 5 or 6 minutes. Transfer to the mixing bowl. Add the tomatoes, scallions, thyme, and extra-virgin olive oil, and thoroughly combine.

Variation: Add ½ cup diced, cooked andouille sausage.

Serving suggestions: With ham or shrimp.

Yield: About 2 cups   **Heat:** 6-7

≈ PRETTY 'N' PEPPERY SALSA ≈

1 yellow tomato, seeded and diced
1 red tomato, seeded and diced
1 green tomato, seeded and diced
10 leaves Oriental mustard greens,
stems removed and finely julienned
18 arugula leaves
2 tablespoons La Carreta red chile apple cider vinegar
or other cider vinegar
1 tablespoon virgin olive oil
⅓ teaspoon salt
¼ teaspoon freshly ground black pepper
1 cup edible nasturtium blossoms, for garnish

Thoroughly combine the tomatoes, greens, vinegar, oil, salt and pepper in a mixing bowl. Garnish with the nasturtium blossoms.

Serving suggestions: With chicken or quail.

Yield: About 1¾ cups   **Heat:** 1-2

≈ CHAYOTE SALSA ≈

1 chayote, peeled and diced (about ¾ cup)
¾ cup diced honeydew melon
¾ cup diced fennel root
2 teaspoons chopped fennel tops
1 tablespoon unseasoned rice wine vinegar
1 teaspoon green habanero chile sauce (such as El Yucateca)
1 tablespoon fresh lime juice
⅛ teaspoon sugar
⅛ teaspoon salt

Thoroughly combine all the ingredients together in a mixing bowl.

Note: Chayote, also known as mirliton, is native to Mexico and the Southwest. It is a pear-shaped, pale green fruit that is commonly used like a squash. It has a delicate flavor and a crisp, fine texture.

Serving suggestions: With chicken or pork.

Yield: About 2 cups   **Heat:** 5-6

≈ CARROT AND BLACK OLIVE ≈ SALSA

6 carrots, finely grated (about 2 cups)
10 Kalamata or Niçoise olives, pitted and minced
¼ cup extra-virgin olive oil
2 tablespoons fresh lemon juice
1½ teaspoons finely minced lemon zest
¾ teaspoon cayenne powder
¼ teaspoon salt

Thoroughly combine all the ingredients together in a mixing bowl.
Serving suggestions: With chicken or tuna.
Yield: About 2 cups   **Heat:** 5

≈ JICAMA SALSA ≈

1 small jicama, peeled and diced (about 1 cup)
8 radishes, diced
¾ cup peeled and diced cucumber
2½ tablespoons fresh lime juice
2 tablespoons diced sweet red onion
¾ teaspoon ground árbol chile
2 teaspoons minced fresh basil
⅔ teaspoon salt
⅛ teaspoon sugar

Thoroughly combine all the ingredients together in a mixing bowl.
Serving suggestions: With steak, or as a soup garnish.
Yield: About 2 cups   **Heat:** 3-4

Nuts and seeds have been used as foods since ancient times. They are nutritious and flavorful, and they store well. They are natural partners for herbs; from the pipians of the early Latin cultures to the pestos of the Mediterranean, these ingredients have been combined as condiments to enrich other foods.

≈

NUT, SEED AND HERB

S A L S A S

≈

~~~~~~~

≈ NEW MEXICAN PIÑON SALSA ≈

**2 dried New Mexico red chiles,
seeded and stemmed
3 cups peanut oil
6 tortillas (preferably 3 blue and 3 yellow),
sliced into thin strips, about 1½ inches long
2 tablespoons fresh lime juice
½ teaspoon salt
2 tablespoons piñons (pine nuts), toasted**

Toast the chiles and rehydrate them in 1 cup of warm water (page 144). Slice into thin strips, about 1½ inches long. Transfer to a mixing bowl.

In a deep-fryer or saucepan, heat the oil to 375 degrees. Sprinkle the tortillas with lime juice and fry in the hot oil for 15 seconds or until crisp but not browned. Remove the strips, drain, and sprinkle with salt. Transfer to the mixing bowl, add the pine nuts, and thoroughly combine.

Serving suggestions: As a garnish for soups or salads, or as a side dish with eggs.

Yield: About 2¾ cups   **Heat:** 5-6

~~~~~~~

CILANTRO AND
≈ OVEN-ROASTED TOMATO ≈
SALSA

**15 Roma tomatoes, oven-roasted and diced (about 1½ cups)
3 tablespoons finely chopped fresh cilantro
1½ teaspoons minced serrano chiles, with seeds
2 teaspoons fresh lime juice**

Thoroughly combine all the ingredients together in a mixing bowl.

Serving suggestions: With grilled tuna or pasta, or as a sandwich spread.

Yield: About 1½ cups   **Heat:** 4

~~~~~~~

≈ THAI PEANUT SALSA ≈

3 tablespoons roasted shallots
1 cup canned coconut milk
½ cup smooth peanut butter
2 teaspoons palm sugar or light brown sugar
2 teaspoons cayenne powder
1 tablespoon Oriental fish sauce
1 tablespoon lemon tamari soy sauce
2 tablespoons fresh lime juice

Place all the ingredients in a food processor or blender and blend until smooth.

Note: If lemon tamari is unavailable, substitute with 2 teaspoons tamari soy sauce and 1 teaspoon fresh lemon juice.

Serving suggestions: With chicken or fish, or with satays.

Yield: About 1¼ cups   **Heat:** 6

≈ GROUND NUT SALSA ≈

6 dried árbol chiles, stemmed and seeded
4 dried New Mexico red chiles, stemmed and seeded
1 cup dry-roasted peanuts
2 Roma tomatoes, blackened
1 red bell pepper, roasted and roughly chopped
1 teaspoon toasted ground coriander seed
1 teaspoon toasted ground cumin seed
3 tablespoons ginger juice, squeezed in a garlic press
3 tablespoons fresh lemon juice
2 tablespoons molasses
2 tablespoons peanut oil
1 teaspoon salt

Toast the chiles together and rehydrate them in 3 cups of warm water (page 144). Drain the chiles, reserving 2 cups of the water, and transfer to a food processor or blender. If it is not bitter, add the reserved chile water; otherwise, add 2 cups plain water. Add the remaining ingredients and purée until smooth.

Serving suggestions: With chicken or grilled snapper.

Yield: About 3 cups   **Heat:** 9-10

~~~

≈ HOJA SANTA SALSA ≈

3 yellow tomatoes (about 1 pound), seeded, and diced
1 large yellow bell pepper, roasted, peeled, seeded, and diced
1 tablespoon minced fresh hoja santa (less than ½ leaf)
1½ teaspoons Coyote Cocina Howlin' Hot Sauce
or other Scotch bonnet chile sauce
2 teaspoons fresh lime juice
½ teaspoon salt
Pinch of sugar

Thoroughly combine all the ingredients together in a mixing bowl.
Note: *Hoja santa*, or *yerba santa*, is also known as the root beer plant because of its flavor. It has large, almost heart-shaped green leaves and grows up to 10 feet high. In Mexico it is popular as a digestive stimulant.
Serving suggestions: With salmon or chicken.
Yield: About 2 cups   **Heat:** 4

~~~

≈ MINT AND CARAMELIZED SHALLOT SALSA ≈

2 tablespoons peanut oil
10 shallots, peeled and sliced into thin rings
1 tablespoon fresh ginger, (preferably young,
Hawaiian ginger) finely minced
½ bunch fresh mint, minced (about ¼ cup)
½ cup minced fresh pineapple
2 tablespoons fresh (or canned) pineapple juice
1 teaspoon minced red Thai chiles, with seeds,
or 1½ teaspoons minced red serrano chiles
¾ teaspoon sugar
1 teaspoon Oriental fish sauce
2 tablespoons unseasoned rice wine vinegar

Heat the peanut oil in a sauté pan or skillet and sauté the shallots over medium-high heat for about 10 minutes, or until browned. Transfer to a mixing bowl and allow to cool. Add the remaining ingredients and thoroughly combine.
Serving suggestions: With pork or chicken.
Yield: About ¾ cup   **Heat:** 5-6

~~~

≈ POBLANO PESTO ≈

¾ cup pumpkin seeds
¼ cup canola oil
5 poblano chiles
1 cup loosely packed cilantro leaves
1 tablespoon virgin olive oil
2 tablespoons fresh lime juice
½ teaspoon salt

Toast the pumpkin seeds and let cool. Heat the canola oil in a skillet and when almost smoking, turn the poblanos in the hot oil for 45 seconds until blistered but not blackened. Transfer to a bowl, cover with plastic wrap, and let steam for 10 minutes.

Peel and seed the poblanos, place in a food processor with the toasted pumpkin seeds, and chop for 1 minute. Add the cilantro and blend for 1 minute. Add the olive oil, lime juice, and salt, and run for 30 seconds longer, or until smooth.

Serving suggestions: With pasta or rabbit.

Yield: About 2 cups   **Heat:** 5

≈ RED CHILE PIPIÁN SALSA ≈

2 dried ancho chiles, stemmed and seeded
1 dried guajillo chile, stemmed and seeded
1 dried árbol chile, stemmed and seeded
1 dried chipotle chile, stemmed
2 Roma tomatoes, blackened
¾ cup dry-roasted peanuts
1 clove roasted garlic
1 teaspoon extra-virgin olive oil
1 teaspoon sugar
¾ teaspoon ground canela
¼ teaspoon ground allspice
½ teaspoon salt

Toast the ancho, guajillo, and árbol chiles together and rehydrate them together with the chipotle in 2 cups of warm water (page 144). Drain the chiles, reserving ¾ cup of the water, and transfer to a food processor or blender. If it is not bitter, add the reserved chile water; otherwise, add ¾ cup plain water. Add the remaining ingredients to the food processor or blender, and purée until smooth.

Note: A canned chipotle chile can be substituted for the dried chipotle. It does not need to be toasted and rehydrated.

Serving suggestions: With chicken or lamb.

Yield: About 1¾ cups   **Heat:** 5

≈ HERB PIPIÁN SALSA ≈

3 serrano chiles, stemmed
2 poblano chiles, roasted and seeded
¼ cup piñons (pine nuts), toasted
¼ cup pumpkin seeds, toasted
1 clove roasted garlic
4 leaves Romaine lettuce
5 fresh epazote leaves
1 cup radish tops
1 small bunch fresh cilantro, stemmed
2 tablespoons chopped fresh basil
¼ teaspoon salt
¼ teaspoon sugar
½ cup water

Place all the ingredients in a food processor or blender and purée until smooth.

Serving suggestions: With duck or firm-fleshed fish such as tuna or swordfish.

Yield: About 2 cups   **Heat:** 6-7

≈ TEJAS SUNFLOWER SEED SALSA ≈

1 pound tomatillos, blackened
½ cup sun-dried tomatoes (in oil), drained
½ cup sunflower seeds, toasted
¼ cup fresh grapefruit juice
1 tablespoon minced grapefruit zest
½ teaspoon salt
½ teaspoon cayenne powder or árbol chile powder
¼ teaspoon sugar

Place the tomatillos and sun-dried tomatoes in a food processor or blender, and blend together. Then add the remaining ingredients and blend, leaving the mixture slightly chunky and textured.

Serving suggestions: With duck or pork.

Yield: About 2 cups   **Heat:** 4

I think of the sea as our other great garden,
bestowing upon us as great a wealth of
life-sustaining riches as does the earth itself.
The simplicity and versatility of seafood
make it a wonderful ingredient for salsas.
You should only use seafood that is
absolutely fresh, and if you are in any doubt
about the quality, wait until next time.

≈≈≈≈≈≈≈

≈ LOBSTER SALSA ≈

1 cup chopped cooked lobster tail and claw meat (2 lobsters)
2 oranges, peeled, seeded, and cut into sections
1 lime, peeled, seeded, and cut into sections
½ grapefruit, peeled, seeded, and cut into sections
1 tablespoon julienned fresh basil
1½ teaspoons Coyote Cocina Howlin' Hot Sauce
or other Scotch bonnet chile sauce

Thoroughly combine all the ingredients together in a mixing bowl.

Serving suggestions: On crispy tostadas, with salads, or as a brunch side dish.

Yield: About 1¾ cups   **Heat:** 5

≈≈≈≈≈≈≈

≈ CRAB AND CORN SALSA ≈

1 ear corn
¼ cup water
1 teaspoon sugar
¼ cup canola oil
1 poblano chile
4 ounces crabmeat
½ red bell pepper, seeded and diced
1 serrano chile, minced, with seeds
1 teaspoon chopped fresh marjoram
1 tablespoon fresh lime juice

With a sharp knife, cut the corn kernels from the cob (about ¾ cup). Bring the water to a boil in a saucepan, add the corn and sugar, and blanch for 1 minute. Drain, and transfer the corn to a mixing bowl.

Heat the canola oil in a skillet, and when almost smoking, turn the poblano in the hot oil for 45 seconds until blistered but not blackened. Transfer to a bowl, cover with plastic wrap, and let steam for 10 minutes. Peel, seed, and dice the poblano, and transfer to the mixing bowl. Add the remaining ingredients and thoroughly combine.

Serving suggestions: On tostadas, or as a soup garnish.

Yield: About 2¼ cups   **Heat:** 3-4

≈≈≈≈≈≈≈

≈SMOKED SHRIMP SALSA≈

1 cup shelled small smoked shrimp (5 ounces)
3 Roma tomatoes, blackened and chopped
2 chipotle chiles en adobo, julienned
2½ tablespoons adobo sauce
2 tablespoons fresh lemon juice
1½ tablespoons chopped fresh cilantro
⅛ teaspoon toasted ground cumin

Thoroughly combine all the ingredients together in a mixing bowl.

Note: Smoked shrimp are available in most gourmet or specialty stores; also see the Sources list (page 147).

Serving suggestions: With grilled fish, or as a soup garnish, sandwich filling, or pizza topping.

Yield: About 1½ cups   **Heat:** 7

≈SANTA FE SHRIMP SALSA≈

1¼ pounds shrimp
2 tablespoons peanut oil
1½ tablespoons minced garlic
1½ tablespoons finely minced fresh ginger
¼ teaspoon salt
½ cup fresh orange juice
1 tablespoon La Carreta chile apple cider vinegar
or other cider vinegar
2 tablespoons minced, seeded red bell pepper
2 tablespoons minced, seeded yellow bell pepper
3 tablespoons diced cucumber
2 tablespoons minced fresh basil
1 tablespoon Coyote Cocina Howlin' Hot Sauce
or other Scotch bonnet chile sauce
1 teaspoon ginger juice, squeezed in a garlic press

Remove the heads and tails of the shrimp, peel and devein. Heat the oil in a sauté pan or skillet until just smoking. Add the garlic and ginger and sauté over high heat for 2 minutes, until browned. Add the shrimp and salt, and sauté for 2 minutes longer over high heat until the shrimp are just pink and cooked through. Add the orange juice and vinegar and cook for 30 seconds, stirring. Transfer to a mixing bowl, add the remaining ingredients, and thoroughly combine.

Serving suggestions: With grilled fish such as halibut or sea bass, or with pasta.

Yield: About 3 cups   **Heat:** 5-6

≈ SCALLOP SALSA ≈

1 tablespoon virgin olive oil
8 ounces sea scallops
3 chipotle chiles en adobo
3 Roma tomatoes, seeded and diced
1 avocado, peeled, pitted, and diced
⅓ cup diced cucumber
1 tablespoon fresh lime juice

Heat the olive oil in a sauté pan or skillet and sear the scallops over high heat for 2 minutes, until cooked through. Slice the scallops in half and then each half into quarters, and transfer to a mixing bowl.

Rinse the chipotles with water and julienne into thin strips. Add to the mixing bowl together with the tomatoes, avocado, cucumber, and lime juice, and thoroughly combine.

Serving suggestions: With salads or as a picnic dish.

Yield: About 2¼ cups   **Heat:** 4

SEAWEED AND ≈ RED CHILE SALSA ˜

1¼ cups cooked green seaweed
2 tablespoons fresh lemon juice
Zest of 2 lemons, minced
1 red Fresno chile or red jalapeño, thinly sliced
into rings, with seeds

Thoroughly combine all the ingredients together in a mixing bowl.

Note: Precooked seaweed is available at most Oriental markets, Japanese markets in particular.

Serving suggestions: With grilled oysters or barbecued fish.

Yield: About 1½ cups   **Heat:** 6

≈ MUSSEL SALSA ≈

1 pound small black mussels, debearded and cleaned
4 cloves garlic, sliced
½ cup white wine, such as Chardonnay
½ cup water
1 tablespoon freshly ground black pepper
1 bay leaf
1 large potato, peeled and diced
½ leek, white part only, sliced
1½ tablespoons virgin olive oil
1½ tablespoons fresh lime juice
1 tablespoon chopped fresh Italian parsley

Place the mussels in a large saucepan with the garlic, wine, water, pepper, and bay leaf, and bring to a boil. Steam, covered, for 5 minutes until the mussels open (discard any that do not open). Remove the mussel meat from the shells and transfer to a mixing bowl. Reduce the cooking liquid to ½ cup and set aside.

Blanch the diced potato in 1 quart boiling salted water for 8 to 10 minutes until tender. Drain in a sieve or strainer, shock under cold running water, and transfer to the mixing bowl. Blanch the leek in 2 cups boiling water for 2 to 3 minutes, until al dente, and transfer to the mixing bowl.

Place the reserved cooking liquid in a blender and blend with the olive oil and lime juice. Add to the mixing bowl with the parsley, and thoroughly combine.

Serving suggestions: As a brunch dish or with pasta.

Yield: About 2 cups   **Heat:** 2

≈ CABO CRAB SALSA ≈

8 ounces crabmeat
3 tomatillos, husked, rinsed, and diced
2 serrano chiles, minced, with seeds
2 teaspoons minced fresh epazote
1 tablespoon minced fresh basil
2 tablespoons extra-virgin olive oil
2 tablespoons fresh lime juice
¼ teaspoon salt

Thoroughly combine all the ingredients together in a mixing bowl.

Serving suggestions: With grilled swordfish or halibut, or as a trout stuffing. Can also be served with cold pasta, or as a brunch side dish or soup garnish.

Yield: About 1¾ cups   **Heat:** 5

≈ MANILA CLAM SALSA ≈

2 pounds Manila clams
½ cup white wine
2 tablespoons virgin olive oil
2 tablespoons minced shallots
2 cloves garlic, sliced
5 serrano chiles, roasted and minced, with seeds
4 Roma tomatoes, seeded and diced
1 tablespoon minced fresh cilantro
1 teaspoon finely minced fresh marjoram
2 tablespoons fresh lime juice

Place the clams in a large saucepan with the wine, 1 tablespoon of the oil, shallots, and garlic, and bring to a boil. Steam, covered, for 10 to 12 minutes until the clams open (discard any that do not open).

Reserve the liquid, shell the clams, and transfer the clam meat to a mixing bowl. Add 2 tablespoons of the reserved liquid, the remaining 1 tablespoon oil, and the rest of the ingredients, and thoroughly combine.

Serving suggestions: With hot or cold pasta, or as a soup garnish.

Yield: About 2 cups   **Heat:** 6

≈ SMOKED SALMON SALSA ≈

4 ounces smoked salmon, finely diced
3 tablespoons finely diced sun-dried tomatoes (in oil)
¾ cup finely diced fennel bulb
3 tablespoons chopped fennel tops
2 tablespoons fresh lemon juice
¾ teaspoon freshly ground black pepper
¼ teaspoon cayenne powder

Thoroughly combine all the ingredients together in a mixing bowl.

Serving suggestions: On top of eggs, as a soup garnish (for tomato soup in particular), or with pasta.

Yield: About 1¾ cups   **Heat:** 3-4

From the craggy mesas of the Southwest, to the souks of North Africa, the vibrant tapas bars of Spain, the buzzing bazaars of India, and the far reaches of the Orient comes this eclectic group of salsas. They feature some unusual ingredients and recombinations of traditional flavors. Each one is a culinary adventure that will take you to far-away places and help transform the most mundane of meals.

EXOTIC

SALSAS

≈ CURRIED SALSA ≈

1 tablespoon peanut oil
¼ cup finely diced onion
1 teaspoon minced garlic
1½ tablespoons curry powder
1 teaspoon cayenne powder
½ teaspoon toasted ground coriander seed
⅛ teaspoon toasted ground cumin
½ pineapple, peeled, cored, chopped, and puréed (about ¾ cup)
⅓ cup fresh or canned pineapple juice
3 Roma tomatoes, blackened and chopped
2 teaspoons brown sugar
1 tablespoon of ginger juice, squeezed in a garlic press
4 bananas (about 1 pound), peeled and diced (about 2 cups)

Heat the oil in a large sauté pan or skillet, add the onion, garlic, curry powder, cayenne, coriander and cumin, and sauté over medium heat for 5 minutes, stirring occasionally. Add the puréed pineapple, pineapple juice, tomatoes, sugar, and ginger juice, and sauté for 10 minutes longer over medium heat until thickened. Let cool, transfer to a mixing bowl, and fold in the bananas.

Serving suggestions: With rice (as a vegetarian curry), lamb, or goat.

Yield: About 3¼ cups   **Heat:** 8-9

≈ COUSCOUS SALSA ≈

1¼ cups water
1½ teaspoons salt
1 tablespoon virgin olive oil
1 cup dried couscous
3 tablespoons raisins
2 red bell peppers, roasted, peeled, seeded, and diced
2 fresh New Mexico green chiles, roasted,
peeled, seeded, and diced
½ cup diced yellow tomato
2 tablespoons fresh lemon juice
2 tablespoons minced fresh cilantro
1½ teaspoons toasted ground coriander
¾ teaspoon toasted ground cumin
¾ teaspoon cayenne powder

In a pan, bring 1 cup of the water and 1 teaspoon salt to a boil. Remove from the heat. In a separate pan or skillet, heat the olive oil over medium heat, add the couscous, and quickly stir to coat it with the oil. Add the hot water, remove from the heat, cover the pan, and let sit for 5 minutes. Stir with a whisk to fluff up. Transfer to a mixing bowl.

Plump the raisins in remaining water, about 2 minutes. Drain, and add the raisins to the mixing bowl together with the remaining ½ teaspoon salt and the rest of the ingredients, and thoroughly combine.

Note: Couscous is a grain-like cereal made from semolina. It is a staple dish of North Africa, where it is usually served in combination with a hearty stew. Couscous is available in most large supermarkets or in specialty stores.

Serving suggestions: With lamb or grilled fish, especially snapper.

Yield: About 3 cups   **Heat:** 3-4

≈ *132* ≈

≈ KIM CHEE SALSA ≈

1 quart water
2 tablespoons plus ¼ teaspoon salt
4 cups chopped Napa cabbage, bok choy,
or Oriental mustard greens
1 teaspoon minced garlic
¾ cup sliced scallions, green and white parts
1 teaspoon árbol chile powder, or cayenne
1 tablespoon Oriental toasted sesame oil (rayu)
1 teaspoon of ginger juice, squeezed in a garlic press

In a large saucepan, bring the water and 2 tablespoons of the salt to a boil. Add the cabbage or other greens, and cook for 30 seconds while stirring, until wilted. Drain, let cool, and transfer to a mixing bowl. Add the remaining ingredients and thoroughly combine.

Serving suggestions: With barbecued foods (especially ribs), Chinese potstickers, fish tacos, or sea bass.

Yield: About 2¼ cups   **Heat:** 9

≈ JAPANESE SALSA ≈

1 tablespoon water
4 packed cups fresh spinach
1 teaspoon julienned red pickled ginger
½ teaspoon pure red chile powder, preferably New Mexican
2 teaspoons toasted white sesame seeds
12 thin slices peeled and julienned daikon
1 teaspoon unseasoned rice wine vinegar
¼ cup toasted nori sheets, cut into 1-inch long julienne strips

In a large sauté pan or skillet, heat the water and wilt the spinach over medium-high heat for about 1 minute. Let cool, chop, and transfer to a mixing bowl.

Sprinkle the remaining ingredients in layers over the spinach, starting with the ginger, then the chile powder, sesame seeds, daikon, and vinegar, and finishing with the nori.

Note: Nori is dried Japanese seaweed that is pressed into thin sheets. It is commonly used to wrap sushi, and like the pickled ginger, it is available in Oriental markets. Daikon is a crispy, white Oriental root vegetable very similar to radish.

Serving suggestions: With cold rice, or as a side dish with Chinese or Japanese food.

Yield: About 1 cup   **Heat:** 3

≈ WILD RICE AND QUINOA SALSA ≈

½ cup wild rice
3 cups water
1 tablespoon plus ½ teaspoon salt
⅓ cup quinoa
1 tablespoon peanut oil
1¼ cups diced wild mushrooms, such as chanterelles, morels
or portobellos, or domestic mushrooms
½ teaspoon salt
¼ teaspoon freshly ground black pepper
1 large clove garlic, minced
2 tablespoons chopped fresh Italian parsley
3 tablespoons toasted pumpkin seeds
1 tablespoon pumpkin seed oil (or walnut oil)
1 teaspoon adobo sauce

Rinse the rice and place in a saucepan with 2 cups water. Bring to
a boil and stir with a wooden spoon. Reduce the heat and simmer,
covered, for 45 minutes to 1 hour, until tender and the water has
evaporated. If the water evaporates before the rice is done, add
more as needed. Remove from heat and let stand for 5 minutes.

In a separate saucepan, bring the remaining 1 cup water and 1
tablespoon salt to a boil, add the quinoa, reduce the heat, cover, and
cook until tender and the water has evaporated, about 12 minutes.

Heat the peanut oil in a large sauté pan or skillet, season the
mushrooms with ¼ teaspoon salt and the pepper, and sauté with
the garlic over medium-high heat for 1 minute. Transfer to a mixing bowl, add the cooked rice and quinoa, the remaining ¼ teaspoon salt and the rest of the ingredients, and thoroughly combine.
Note: Quinoa is a South American grain that was used by the Incas.
Often referred to as a "complete grain," it contains the highest protein of any grain. Quinoa is growing rapidly in popularity and is available in health food stores as well as some large supermarkets.
Pumpkin seed oil is also available at most health food stores.
Serving suggestions: With grilled meats, especially lamb, venison,
and buffalo.
Yield: About 2 cups   **Heat:** 1

≈ ROASTED COCONUT SALSA ≈

1 cup dried coconut
1 tablespoon sugar
2 tablespoons peanut oil
2 cloves garlic, sliced
5 ounces shallots (about 7), peeled and sliced
1 tablespoon pure red chile powder, preferably New Mexico red
1½ teaspoons árbol chile powder
4 ounces cashew nuts, toasted and ground (about ½ cup)

Preheat the oven to 250 degrees. Combine the coconut and sugar,
spread on a baking sheet, and toast in the oven for about 2 minutes or until lightly browned; shake 3 or 4 times while toasting.
Transfer to a mixing bowl.

Heat the oil in a sauté pan or skillet and sauté the garlic and
shallots over medium-low heat for about 30 minutes or until well
browned. Add to the mixing bowl together with the remaining
ingredients and thoroughly combine.
Serving suggestions: As a garnish for rice dishes, with Indian or
Southeast Asian food, or sprinkled over Indonesian satays.
Yield: About 1¾ cups   **Heat:** 8-9

≈ SALSA ROMESCO ≈

10 Roma tomatoes, oven-roasted
2 red bell peppers, roasted, peeled, seeded, and roughly chopped
3 cloves garlic
½ cup toasted sliced almonds
2 teaspoons cayenne powder
1 teaspoon salt
2 tablespoons sherry vinegar
1 tablespoon fresh lemon juice
1 tablespoon virgin olive oil

Place all the ingredients in a food processor or blender and purée.

Variation: Add 1 anchovy filet to the food processor.

Note: This is a classic Spanish salsa.

Serving suggestions: A versatile salsa, good with tortilla chips or as a dip for vegetables; with grilled meats, fish or eggs; or as a soup garnish.

Yield: About 1¾ cups   **Heat:** 5-6

≈ SMOKY BARBECUE SALSA ≈

1 cup barbecue sauce, your favorite kind
2 cups peeled shallots, or small white boiling onions
2 tablespoons chipotle chile purée (page 145)
2 tablespoons molasses
1 tablespoon pure maple syrup
2 tablespoons red wine vinegar
¼ cup water
2 small ears corn

Place the barbecue sauce, shallots, chipotle purée, molasses, maple syrup, vinegar and water in a saucepan, and bring to a boil. Reduce the heat and simmer, covered, for 1 hour. Add more water as necessary to prevent the mixture getting too thick.

With a sharp knife cut the corn kernels from the cob (about 1 cup). Heat a large, heavy-bottomed sauté pan or skillet over high heat until almost smoking. Place no more than 2 layers of the corn kernels in the pan at a time, and dry-roast for 4 to 5 minutes until smoky and dark, tossing continuously. Transfer to a mixing bowl, add the barbecue mixture, and thoroughly combine.

Serving suggestions: With chicken or steak.

Yield: About 2 cups   **Heat:** 5

≈ TABBOULEH-PARSLEY- ≈ MINT SALSA

⅔ cup dried tabbouleh (5 ounces)
1 cup water
3 Roma tomatoes, seeded and diced
2 serrano chiles, minced, with seeds
2 tablespoons finely minced red onion
½ teaspoon finely minced garlic
¼ cup minced fresh parsley
1 tablespoon finely minced lemon zest
¼ cup fresh lemon juice
1½ tablespoons virgin olive oil
⅔ teaspoon salt

Place the tabbouleh and water in a mixing bowl and let sit for 30 minutes to allow the tabbouleh to absorb the water. Add the remaining ingredients and thoroughly combine.

Note: Tabbouleh, made from bulghur wheat, is an important element of Middle Eastern cuisine. It can be bought pre-packaged from specialty markets, larger supermarkets, or Middle Eastern stores.

Serving suggestions: With grilled chicken, lamb, or fish.

Yield: About 3 cups   **Heat:** 4

≈ NOPALES CACTUS SALSA ≈

2 dried árbol chiles, broken up by hand
2 cloves garlic, sliced
1 tablespoon black peppercorns
2 tablespoons cracked coriander seed
2 sprigs fresh thyme
½ cup La Carreta cilantro apple cider vinegar
or other cider vinegar
Juice of 2 lemons
2 cups water
8 ounces cactus pads (about 4), dethorned
and edges peeled, cut into large dice
8 radishes, sliced
3 oranges, peeled, seeded, and cut into sections
2 tablespoons fresh orange juice
½ red bell pepper, roasted, peeled, seeded,
and cut into strips
½ teaspoon árbol chile powder or cayenne powder
¼ teaspoon salt

Place the chiles, garlic, peppercorns, coriander, thyme, vinegar, lemon juice and water in a large saucepan and bring to a boil. Reduce the heat and simmer, uncovered, for 10 minutes. Strain and return the liquid to a clean pan (discard the solids). Add the cactus to the liquid and cook for 1 minute over high heat. Drain, and transfer the cactus to a mixing bowl. Add the remaining ingredients and thoroughly combine.

Note: The pads of the nopal cactus (also called *nopales*) can be obtained from Latin markets or specialty stores that carry Southwestern products. Wear garden gloves when you remove the spines.

Serving suggestions: With grilled meats, especially lamb or beef.

Yield: About 2 cups   **Heat:** 4

≈COOKING TECHNIQUES≈

Blackening Tomatoes and Tomatillos

This gives tomatoes and tomatillos a more rustic, robust, and complex flavor. Remove the stems (tomatillos should also be husked and rinsed) and place on a rack under a broiler or over a gas flame until the skins blister, crack, and blacken. This technique replicates the traditional method of blackening them over open fires or grills. A hand-held butane torch can also be used. Do not over-blacken, or a bitter taste will result.

Oven-Roasting Tomatoes

This technique removes the excess moisture from the tomatoes and concentrates the flavor. Preheat the oven to 250 degrees. Cut the tomatoes in half and place cut side up on a wire rack or on a baking sheet. Sprinkle with a little salt. Roast in the oven for about 3 hours. If desired, you can place a sliver or two of fresh garlic in the middle of each tomato half (discard the garlic when the tomatoes are roasted). If not using immediately, the tomatoes can be stored in a jar, in olive oil.

Roasting and Peeling Fresh Chiles and Bell Peppers

Roasting chiles or bell peppers (which are botanically also chiles) concentrates their natural sugars and brings out more complex, robust, smoky flavors. This technique also facilitates peeling the tough skin which can be bitter.

Place the chiles or bell peppers on a wire rack over an open gas flame, on a grill, or under a broiler; a hand-held butane torch can also be used. Blister and blacken the skins all over, without burning the flesh. Transfer to a bowl, cover with plastic wrap or a clean kitchen towel, and let steam for 15 to 20 minutes. You can then remove the skin with your fingers or with the tip of a knife. Remove the seeds and internal ribs if the recipe calls for it. Removing the seeds and membranes will diminish the heat of chiles.

When it is important to retain the color of the chiles, it is preferable to blister them in hot oil instead of blackening them. Heat $\frac{1}{4}$ cup canola oil until just smoking, and turn the chile in the oil for 45 seconds. Transfer to a bowl, cover with plastic wrap, and let steam for 10 minutes. The chile can then be handled as above.

After you have handled chiles, do not touch your face or eyes until you have thoroughly washed your hands. If you have sensitive skin, wear rubber gloves when handling chiles.

Roasting Corn

As with chiles, this technique provides additional flavor dimensions, especially an appealing smokiness that particularly enhances the natural flavor of corn. Cut the corn kernels from the cobs with a sharp knife. Heat a large, heavy-bottomed sauté pan or skillet over high heat until almost smoking. Place no more than two layers of the corn kernels in the pan at a time, and dry-roast for 4 to 5 minutes until smoky and dark, tossing continuously.

Roasting Garlic

Roasted garlic is mellower, sweeter, and more subtle in flavor than raw, fresh garlic. Place unpeeled garlic cloves in a heavy-bottomed cast-iron skillet and dry-roast over low heat for 30 to 40 minutes, until the garlic softens. Shake the skillet occasionally. Alternatively, roast the garlic cloves in the oven for 20 to 30 minutes at 350 degrees. When roasted, you should be able to squeeze the garlic out of the cloves.

Roasting Shallots

Preheat the oven to 350 degrees. Place the unpeeled shallots on a baking sheet and roast for 30 to 35 minutes. Squeeze the shallots out of their skins and mince if desired.

Sectioning Citrus Fruit

With a sharp paring knife, cut about $\frac{1}{2}$ inch off each end of the fruit and peel off all the skin and white pith. Cut out sections from the fruit segments of the desired thickness.

Toasting and Rehydrating Dried Chiles

It is most common to toast and rehydrate dried chiles before puréeing them in Southwestern cuisine. Stem and seed the dried chiles, and dry-roast in a single layer in dry cast-iron skillet, or on a baking sheet in a 250 degree oven, for 2 to 3 minutes. Shake occasionally and do not allow to burn or blacken, or the chiles will taste bitter. Transfer the chiles to a bowl and add enough hot water just to cover. Let stand for about 20 minutes until they are rehydrated and soft.

Toasting Dried Herbs and Spices

Toasting gives herbs and spices a more intense flavor. To toast herbs such as oregano and spices such as coriander and cumin, place in a dry skillet over low heat. Toast for about 1 minute or until fragrant, stirring frequently. Do not scorch or they will taste bitter.

Toasting Nuts

Toasting nuts brings out the natural richness and full flavors of nuts, like roasting coffee beans. Place in a hot dry skillet and toast over medium heat for 5 to 7 minutes until lightly browned, stirring occasionally. Smaller nuts, such as pine nuts, or sliced almonds, will take 3 to 5 minutes. Alternatively, nuts may be toasted on a cookie sheet in a 250 degree oven for 5 to 10 minutes, depending on the type of nut.

Toasting Seeds

Toasting seeds, as with nuts, brings out their complex, rich flavors. Place in a hot dry skillet for 2 to 3 minutes over medium-high heat until lightly browned, stirring occasionally. Pumpkin seeds take a little longer (about 4 to 5 minutes), and pop when they are done; remove from heat when the popping subsides.

Cooking Beans

In general, it is not necessary to soak beans before cooking them. Soaking helps soften old beans, but these days, beans tend to be quite fresh, and soaking only loosen the husks, which makes for messy beans. Cook beans in water to cover by at least $1\frac{1}{2}$ inches, simmering uncovered for 45 minutes to 1 hour. Do not add salt until the last 15 minutes or so of cooking: adding before then will make the beans tough.

≈ GLOSSARY ≈

Adobo sauce

The picante sauce made from tomatoes, onions, vinegar and spices in which canned chipotle chiles are packed. Adobo sauce is used in Mexican and Southwestern cuisines to provide both flavor and heat for certain dishes.

Chipotle chiles

Chipotle chiles, usually, are smoked, dried jalapeños, and they are available in dried form or pickled and canned in adobo sauce (chipotle chiles en adobo — see above).

Chipotle chile purée

Made from canned chipotle chiles en adobo (see above). Simply purée the canned chiles with some of the adobo sauce in which the chiles are packed.

Chocolate

See Ibarra chocolate.

Dice

When recipes in this book call for ingredients to be diced, they should be cut into ¼-inch cubes. Fine dice refers to ⅛-inch cubes, large dice to ⅓- or ½-inch cubes.

Epazote

Also known as wormseed or skunkweed. It is a pungent Mexican herb that is becoming increasingly popular in the United States. It can be bought at Latin markets.

Ginger juice

This versatile flavoring is made by squeezing grated ginger through a garlic press. Three tablespoons of grated ginger will yield about 1 tablespoon of ginger juice; 4 ounces will yield about ¼ cup. The pulp should be discarded.

Ibarra chocolate

A Mexican chocolate that is made with cacao, cinnamon, sugar, and ground almonds.

Julienne

Thin, even strips, usually measuring 2 to 3 inches in length and ¼ inch wide.

La Carreta vinegar

This brand is widely available in the Southwest, or see Sources for a mail-order supplier. We use their flavored cider vinegars in many of our salsas. Regular cider vinegar can be substituted.

Olive oil

Olive oil comes in three main grades: pure, virgin, and extra-virgin. The recipes in this book call for either virgin or extra-virgin. Pure olive oil is the most refined of the three grades but is of an inferior quality. Virgin olive oil is the product of the pressurized and heat-assisted second pressing, while extra-virgin, the purest and highest quality oil, is produced from the first (cold) pressing. Extra-virgin olive oil is very low in acidity and is the most flavorful type of olive oil. In some cases, this assertive flavor is desirable in a recipe; in other cases not, as it can overwhelm more delicately flavored ingredients.

Rajas

"Slivers" or "strips" in Spanish. In the Southwest it refers to julienned strips of cooked bell peppers or chiles.

Rice wine vinegar

A Japanese vinegar, available both unseasoned and seasoned (the latter contains sugar and salt). The recipes in this book always call for the unseasoned variety. Most large supermarkets carry both kinds, or get it at Oriental markets or gourmet stores.

Roma tomatoes

We prefer to use roma or plum tomatoes because of their more consistent quality and because of their lower liquid content.

Vinegar *(see specific types)*

Zest

The outer, colored layer of citrus fruit that contains the concentrated aromatic oils. Citrus zesters are invaluable kitchen gadgets, designed to leave behind the bitter white pith that lies beneath the zest.

≈ **SOURCES** ≈

Coyote Cafe General Store

132 West Water Street
Santa Fe, NM 87501
(800) 866-HOWL or
(505) 982-2454

Beans, chiles (including canned chiles en adobo), Ibarra chocolate, canela, spices, herbs, tamarind, La Carreta vinegars, Coyote Cocina Howlin' Hot Sauce.

Elizabeth Berry

Gallina Canyon Ranch
144 Camino Escondido
Santa Fe, NM 87501
(505) 982-4149

Beans and specialty produce.

Los Chileros

P.O.Box 6215
Santa Fe, NM 87501
(505) 471-6967

Chiles.

Bueno Foods

2001 4th Street S.W.
Albuquerque, NM 87102
(505) 243-2722

Chiles, hoja santa, epazote.

B. Riley

607A Juan Tabo Boulevard N.E.
Albuquerque, NM 87123
(505) 275-0902

Herbs (including epazote and hoja santa), fresh mushrooms.

Golden Circle Farms

P.O. Box 2235
Corsicana, TX 75151
(903) 326-4263

Hoja santa and epazote.

Glenn Burns

16158 Hillside Circle
Montverde, FL 34756
(407) 469-4490

Huitlacoche.

La Carreta

Box 70
Dixon, NM 87527
(505) 579-4358

Vinegars, Preserves and sauces

Ducktrap River Fish Farm

57 Little River Drive
Belfast, Maine 04915
(207) 338-6280

Smoked shrimp.

Dean and Deluca

560 Broadway
New York, NY 10012
 (212) 431-1691

Chiles, oils, vinegars, beans.

Monterrey Foods

3939 Caesar Chavez Ave.
Los Angeles, CA 90063
(213) 263-2143

Southwestern and Mexican food products.

Italco Food Products

1340 S. Cherokee Street
Denver, CO 80223
(303) 722-1882

Oils, spices, vinegars.

Taxco Produce

1801 S. Good Latimer Expressway
Dallas, TX 75226
(214) 421-7191

Chiles and other Southwestern ingredients.

In Canada:

Interport Sales LTD.

P.O. Box 51560
West Vancouver, BC
V7T 2X9 Canada

In Europe:

Cool Chile Co.

Dodie Miller Unit 7
34 Bassett Road
London W10 6JL England

*See also
The Great Chile Book
by Mark Miller
(Ten Speed Press)
for ready identification
of chiles used
in this book.*

≈ CONVERSIONS ≈

If you don't live in the U.S., here's a note on equivalent ingredients and measurements.

bell pepper	sweet pepper or capsicum
cantaloupe	rock melon
cilantro	fresh coriander
eggplant	aubergine
Italian parsley	flat-leaf parsley
papaya	pawpaw
Roma tomatoes	plum tomatoes
scallion	spring or green onion
spinach	English spinach
zucchini	courgette

Measuring cups can be found in good kitchen supply stores, but here are some approximate metric and imperial equivalents for some of the ingredients in this book. Unless stated otherwise, all these roughly equal 1 cup.

1 cup	16 tablespoons	250 mL	8 fl oz
1 ounce		30 g	
1 pound		500 g	16 oz
1 quart		1 L	32 fl oz
beans, dried, large/small		185 g/250 g	6 oz/8 oz
bell pepper, roasted		185 g	6 oz
blossoms		120g	4 oz
cabbage, chopped		120 g	4 oz
corn kernels		185 g	6 oz
coconut, dried		90 g	3 oz
cranberries, dried		185 g	6 oz
fennel, chopped		185 g	6 oz
herbs		120 g	4 oz
liquid		250 mL	8 fl oz
mushrooms		120 g	4 oz
nuts, chopped		120 g	4 oz
onions, chopped		185 g	6 oz
pineapple, chopped		120 g	4 oz
raisins		185 g	6 oz
seaweed, cooked		155 g	5 oz
spinach, fresh/cooked		60 g/155 g	2 oz/5 oz
tomatoes, chopped/sundried		250 g/185 g	8 oz/6 oz